THE CHRISTIAN AND THE CULTURE

*A Study of the Challenges Faced by the
Twenty-First Century Christian*

BISHOP ERIC A. LAMBERT JR.

WESTBOW
PRESS®
A DIVISION OF THOMAS NELSON
& ZONDERVAN

Scripture taken from the King James Version of the Bible.

Scripture taken from the Holy Bible, NEW INTERNATIONAL VERSION®. Copyright © 1973, 1978, 1984, 2011 by Biblica, Inc. All rights reserved worldwide. Used by permission. NEW INTERNATIONAL VERSION® and NIV® are registered trademarks of Biblica, Inc. Use of either trademark for the offering of goods or services requires the prior written consent of Biblica US, Inc.

WestBow Press books may be ordered through booksellers or by contacting:

WestBow Press
A Division of Thomas Nelson & Zondervan
1663 Liberty Drive
Bloomington, IN 47403
www.westbowpress.com
1 (866) 928-1240

Because of the dynamic nature of the Internet, any web addresses or links contained in this book may have changed since publication and may no longer be valid. The views expressed in this work are solely those of the author and do not necessarily reflect the views of the publisher, and the publisher hereby disclaims any responsibility for them.

Any people depicted in stock imagery provided by Thinkstock are models, and such images are being used for illustrative purposes only. Certain stock imagery © Thinkstock.

ISBN: 978-1-5127-1568-2 (sc)
ISBN: 978-1-5127-1569-9 (hc)
ISBN: 978-1-5127-1567-5 (e)

Library of Congress Control Number: 2015916943

Print information available on the last page.

WestBow Press rev. date: 11/3/2015

I dedicate this book to my Lord Jesus. Without Him I would not be able to accomplish this work. I want to thank my Pastor and mentor, Rev. Benjamin Smith Sr, a man who taught me what it means to be a genuine servant of the Lord. Special thanks to the congregation at Bethel Deliverance International Church. You are the best and I thank the Lord for the privilege to serve you. Finally, I thank my wife Sheila, our daughter Shaneena and our Godson, Darius. You have been with me through all of the trials and I am thanking and loving you all.

Contents

Introduction

GOD'S CHILDREN ARE UNDER INTENSE pressure to live holy lives. In this postmodern world, we struggle in many areas that bring a degree of frustration to our daily walk with the Lord. We always fight against the worldly culture and the way it invades our lives with doubt, fear, and uncertainty.

In decades past, Christians could withstand this onslaught by just quoting a few Scripture passages and rejoicing. However, in this current climate, we are subjected to more intense battles and are under more intense pressure to stand. The words of the apostle Paul have a greater meaning than ever before.

> Finally, be strong in the Lord and in his mighty power. Put on the full armor of God so that you can take your stand against Satan's schemes. For our struggle is not against flesh and blood, but against the rulers, against the authorities, against the powers of this dark world and against the spiritual forces of evil in the heavenly realms. Therefore put on the full armor of God, so that when the day of evil comes, you may be able to stand your ground, and after you have done everything, to stand. Stand firm then. (Eph. 6:10–14 NIV)

In the past, we were able to find refuge in our local churches, and it seemed as though our Enemy would respect God's house. Now, the battle has infiltrated even that place. Not only our culture but also many of our churches have moved farther away from God and become more ungodly than ever before. People are turning away from the Lord, and the Bible is under attack from every direction. As we observe this departure from the teachings of God's Word, many in the church wonder what is going on. It appears that we are witnessing the fulfillment of the writings of Paul to the church at Thessalonica. He declared that this would be a time of great falling away. "Let no man deceive you by any means: for *that day shall not come*, except there come a falling away first, and that man of sin be revealed, the son of perdition" (2 Thess. 2:3 KJV).

No area of our world is exempt from lawlessness, coldness, and anarchy. These behaviors, combined with the economic pressures that many face, cause believers to pull away from the teachings of God's Word and trust in the false security of the world in which we live. I write this book to call Christians to a higher level of spiritual awareness. Our enemy (Satan) has intensified his attack, and we are forced to stand on the Word of God for support. If we are successful in standing on the Word, then we will be able to resist the wiles (methods) of the Enemy. As believers in the Lord Jesus Christ, we need not succumb to the trappings of this world. Christ has saved us, and then in a grand act of mercy and grace, he has seated the church in heavenly places along with himself. The church is declared to be the righteousness of God, and we are eternally blessed and in positions of spiritual power and authority. The primary challenge in this book is to realize the snare of the wicked and remember to keep yourself pure. It is my prayer that as you read this book, you will find renewed purpose in your walk with God. Do not fear! We are more than conquerors.

Blessings,
Bishop Eric Lambert

PART I

Our Culture Trap

CHAPTER 1

The Call

> I beseech you therefore, brethren, by the mercies of
> God, that ye present your bodies a living sacrifice, holy,
> acceptable unto God, which is your reasonable service.
> And be not conformed to this world: but be ye transformed
> by the renewing of your mind, that ye may prove what is
> that good, and acceptable, and perfect, will of God. (Rom.
> 12:1–2 KJV)

WE BEGIN OUR JOURNEY WITH this passage of Scripture, hoping that it
will challenge your intellect and reignite your desire to connect with the
Lord Jesus. These verses speak of the challenge we face as believers. When
Paul wrote to the saints in Rome, his motive was to help them realize that
Christian life was very different from life in the age to which they belonged.
Christians must always remember that we are to avoid the things of our
generation that may bring us into bondage. Christians are not perfect
persons, but we are to be noticeably different. We dare not become one
with the world to the point of losing our distinctiveness.

Let's begin with Paul's opening statement: "present your bodies as a
living sacrifice." Because our culture views religion as an intruder into

everyday life, you may find it interesting that the apostle begins this chapter with a call to live sacrificially. Many people think God wants us to bring *things* to him. I am sure you have attended church services in which you were encouraged to bring gifts to the Lord. This is an essential component of Christian faith. Yet as we dig deeper into the Word, we find that the gifts that please the Lord most are not our possessions but ourselves. This is why Paul says we are to present our bodies as living sacrifices.

God gave the children of Israel lessons on performing sacrifices. The instructions for sacrifices are prominent in the books of Exodus and Leviticus. In these writings, we see that the Lord takes great care to explain the intricacies of the act of sacrifice. The book of Leviticus lists many types of offerings. Among them are burnt offerings; grain offerings; fellowship offerings; guilt offerings; and the most valuable offering, in my opinion, the sin offering. Each type of offering had specific instructions, and the priests had to follow God's instructions completely. The sacrifices and feasts were meant to remind the Israelites that they were different from those who occupied the pagan lands. However, there were so many different offerings and the instructions were so complicated that the Israelites must have been confused and frustrated by them. Can you imagine doing the same thing once a year, every year, in exactly the same way? One can only imagine that the repetition of these actions became dull.

When people continue to perform the same actions over and over again, the sheer repetition may cause them to develop callous hearts toward the Lord. Consistently performing sacrifices produces a sense of dread and did not create life in the minds of those who had to do those sacrifices. These actions (performing religious duties) may also cause damage to our personal relationships with the Lord. Can you imagine trying to connect with God by killing and burning animals?

For all of you scholars out there, I realize the sacrifices prefigured the Lord Jesus and our future relationship with him. Yet, I cannot help but feel that the sacrifices promoted a religious mind-set, the very type of activity our Lord Jesus came to remove. God has always wanted a personal relationship with his people. He has always wanted to live with us and to be part of our lives. He wants us to love him, personally and intimately, with no strings attached. Perhaps the contrast between the sacrificial system and Jesus's call to a loving, personal relationship was God's way of demonstrating that to us.

Against a similar religious backdrop, Paul addressed the new believers in Rome. While Rome was significant both militarily and culturally, moral values were increasingly scarce. The city was polluted with all types of idolatry and debauchery. This was a culture in decline. Imagine being a Jew in Rome at that time, performing your animal sacrifices and religious observances while others were offering sacrifices to the gods of Rome. It would have been difficult, and you would have struggled with the religious and political climate. Being a scholarly man, Paul, through the inspiration of the Holy Spirit, saw possibilities in this conflict. He told the Christians to stop offering animals to the Lord like their forefathers and to give themselves instead. This is a great encouragement because it reveals the true heart of God toward his people. When we offer ourselves as a living sacrifice, we gain a personal relationship with our Father. Praise the Lord! That is what the Lord wants. No more dead animals, fruit, grain, or things of that nature. In reality, those are just a shadow of the real sacrifice God desires. Yes, he wants us, you, and me, with all of our fears and confusion. He wants to have fellowship with us and bring us into a deeper relationship with him. We are to present our bodies to the Lord and enjoy his presence. Paul tells us that this sacrifice is pleasing to the Lord and acceptable to him. With this sacrifice, there is no uncertainty.

The book of Genesis tells us that Cain offered the Lord something that God did not want. God demanded a personal sacrifice, but Cain was unwilling to give it. As a substitute, Cain offered God a portion of his harvests, and he believed the Lord would accept it. I think the church has been doing exactly the same thing as Cain. We have been offering the Lord our works instead of our bodies. This was the problem with the church at Ephesus. They actually believed the Lord preferred their works to their love. This erroneous thinking resulted in the Lord's rebuke (Rev. 2). When we present our bodies, we know the Lord will accept our offerings. When we give ourselves to the Lord, we feel a sense of victory. In spite of what you think, hear, or feel, God doesn't want your possessions; he wants you.

God has always wanted a relationship with his children. We can only imagine how he felt when the people did not wish to hear from the Lord any longer. The request made to Moses was for him to speak to the Lord on their behalf. This way, they would not have to hear the voice of the Lord and be accountable to him for their actions. I believe this action hurt the Lord. He responded, "O that there were such an heart in them, that they would fear me, and keep all my commandments always, that it might be well with them, and with their children forever" (Deut. 5:29). His cry was clear. God wanted them to have a change of heart. He wants the same thing of us. This is what happens when we spend time developing a relationship with him rather than spend so much time on church work. Nothing brings more joy to the heart of a father than spending time with his children.

I fondly recall times I spent with my daughter. During the summer months when she was a toddler, we would go places together and have fun. The time I spent with my little girl was a source of great pleasure. Now, we recall those times and laugh about them. They were precious, and I will never forget them. Earthly fathers love spending time with their children, and God is no different. He simply wants to spend time with us.

After we are born again, we face the challenge of committing ourselves daily to the Lord. This commitment serves as the beginning of a great personal relationship with God that is the foundation of our Christian life. We must answer God's call to abandon the worldly system that surrounds us and commit ourselves to imitating Christ. We are commanded—yes, commanded—to disconnect ourselves from this human system. Paul's instructions are clear and unmistakable: "Be not conformed to this world." The way Paul uses the word *conformed* is unique. The Greek word used is *suschematizo* (pronounced soos-khay-mat-id'-zo). It carries the idea of being "fashioned alike" or "being conformed to the same pattern (figurative): conform to, fashion one's self according to." Speaking literally, Paul says we are not to fashion ourselves after the world. How do we live in the world without becoming part of it? This is the very challenge Christians have faced throughout the ages.

Paul wrote to the church in Corinth, encouraging them to live differently from the world. Using strong language, he said, "Wherefore come out from among them and be ye separate, says the Lord, and touch not the unclean *thing;* and I will receive you" (2 Cor. 6:17 KJV). The Christians in Corinth had a real problem. They continued to dabble in the behavior to which they had grown accustomed before coming to Christ.

Paul gave explicit directions to the saints in Corinth: separate yourself from the very system that polluted you in the first place.

Later on in the Bible, we learn about the dilemmas faced by the church at Ephesus. They also struggled with fleshly responses that led to spiritual confusion. They wrote to the apostle John and requested help with their issues. John responded in a clear fashion that Christians are to rise above the mediocrity of religion and move into a new realm of perfection. He taught that those who belong to Christ must have a different motivation toward life in general. His counsel is clear.

> Love not the world neither the things *that are* in the world. If any man love the world, the love of the Father is not in him. For all that *is* in the world, the lust of the flesh, and the lust of the eyes, and the pride of life, is not of the Father, but is of the world. And the world passeth away, and the lust thereof: but he that doeth the will of God abideth for ever. (1 John 2:15–17 KJV)

John taught that the Enemy influences our entire social system. The culture is driven by the "pride of life, the lust of the eyes and the lust of the flesh." These actions have always served the purpose of Satan. The things of the kingdom of darkness have become primary in the world, and they provide a strong pull on all in the world, even Christians. These tactics have remained the same for thousands of years. History teaches us that many great civilizations were destroyed because these three vices were active in the world.

Sadly, we see this attitude of depravity in America today. At one time, our culture was dedicated to the principles of the Bible. Now, we are so far away from the principles of God's Word that our seniors hardly recognize this country. Since we possess the knowledge that our nation has abandoned the teachings of the Bible, we must determine not to allow the culture to swallow us and snuff out our lights. We are here to shine for Jesus and demonstrate his power and grace to the world.

The apostle Paul teaches us that we are to grow beyond the limitations of the old lifestyle and embrace the new. He repeatedly tells us to put off the old man and put on the new, which is fashioned after Christ. Paul challenges the believers at Ephesus to a life that will glorify the Lord. He writes, "that ye henceforth walk not as other Gentiles walk, in the vanity of their mind" (Eph. 4:17 KJV). We have also been called to live separately from the ways of the Gentiles. I usually substitute the word *unbelievers* here, because we are Gentiles, but we must strive to live independently from the world. We are called to imitate Christ, *not* the world. This is the primary discipline we face. Paul's words ring in my spirit: "Be not conformed to this world (age), but be transformed by the renewing of the mind." As we examine the Scriptures, we must understand fully what it means to have our minds renewed. Basically, it means to think differently about everything we confront. Unfortunately, this is harder to do than you might think.

Do you remember the phrase "What Would Jesus Do?" (WWJD)? It was all the rage in the Christian world. I remember it well, and it frustrated me a great deal. Many believers thought by simply adding yet another cute saying to their evangelical vocabulary they would capture a generation. However, rather than renewing the mind, it tended to pollute it instead. On one occasion, I was in a bank, and the teller had many items that advertised WWJD. I listened with great interest as she demonstrated an attitude to the customers that did not adequately represent the Lord. The attitude that was displayed did not fulfill the command to "love one another."

When I approached her window, her attitude did not improve. After completing my transaction, I asked her what WWJD stood for, acting as if I did not know. She boasted that it stood for "What Would Jesus Do?" I responded by saying I did not know what he would do, in this case, but I know he would not demonstrate the behavior I had witnessed from her that day. As I left her station, she watched me with a rather curious look.

As this anecdote illustrates, if we are not careful, we can do damage to the cause of Christ by keeping the old mind in place, even if our intentions are good. The call of God is simple: be different! Did you ever wonder what happened to the WWJD craze? Someone became wealthy off the merchandising; that's for sure. In fact, two believers even got into a legal battle over who owned the term! But it did nothing to help the church—or the world—develop the attitude of Christ. Instead, the phrase "What Would Jesus Do?" became just another fad that made Christians look ridiculous in the eyes of the world. I believe that Paul was merely attempting to have believers adjust their way of thinking. The worldview of the Christian is to be in agreement with the Holy Bible. We are called to be a witness of the Lord (Acts 1:8) and to be the light of the world (Matt. 5:14). When we keep these commands in the forefront of our minds, I am sure that we will have the ability to stand against the devices of the devil. When we remember that we are commanded to be the light to the world, we will resist the pull of the worldly system that is designed to weaken our testimonies for Christ. We must review this Apostolic command over and over until it becomes a part of our daily lives.

> I beseech you therefore, brethren, by the mercies of God, that ye present your bodies a living sacrifice, holy, acceptable unto God, *which is* your reasonable service. Be not conformed to this world: but be ye transformed by the renewing of your mind, that ye may prove what is that good, and acceptable, and perfect will of God. (Rom. 12:1–2 KJV)

Let us pray:

Father, please help us develop into people who reflect your love and holiness in these last days. Amen.

Review questions:

1. Do you find yourself pulled into the culture easier than you would like? In what ways?
2. Why do you think that this culture is such a serious challenge for you?
3. How can you resist the temptations and challenges of this culture?

CHAPTER 2

The Challenge

Furthermore then we beseech you, brethren, and exhort you by the Lord Jesus, that as ye have received of us how ye ought to walk and to please God, so ye would abound more and more. For ye know what commandments we gave you by the Lord Jesus. For this is the will of God, even your sanctification, that ye should abstain from fornication: That every one of you should know how to possess his vessel in sanctification and honour. (1 Thess. 4:1–4 KJV)

WITH THESE WORDS, MOST OF us entered into a new life in Christ. We left the altar of God with extreme joy. We anticipated great new lives, and we thought things would get better immediately. We were excited about how great it was to be a Christian, and we could not wait to experience all the things we had heard about from the preachers.

Then it happened—holiness became a reality. For the first time in our new Christian lives, we learned that God demands a lifestyle that brings him glory. Suddenly, things we were accustomed to doing in our everyday life were improper because we realized they polluted our souls. Our response was almost immediate. Faced with the loss of sinful pleasures, the flesh screamed for control. "Wait a minute. I didn't sign up for this! God will have to accept me as I am. What is this new teaching, and when did holiness become a requirement for going to heaven? I want to go to heaven, but on my terms." The one discipline that we have the toughest time dealing with is holiness. The question is, why? That's what this chapter is about.

Our culture teaches us that holiness is not necessary for "religious" purposes. The practice of Holiness is viewed as an old-fashioned teaching. It is not required in the *new* Christian world. Yet our past teachings stated that true holiness and worship are the revelations of the nature and character of God. If we learned anything about God, it is that he is absolutely holy! Just what is holiness, and why is it such a challenge?

To answer that question, we need to go back to the early 1960s. When the Pentecostal movement became an accepted form of worship, we needed something that would separate us from other denominations. Because we rejected ecclesiastical hierarchies and theological idols, we began to take a literal view of the Scriptures as the guideline for our faith in the Lord Jesus. Our theology had many holes in it, yet we thought we were right. For example, I am sure you remember the misunderstood passage in the book of Deuteronomy. This verse states, "The woman shall not wear that which pertaineth unto a man, neither shall a man put on a woman's garment: for all that do so *are* abomination unto the LORD thy God" (Deut. 22:5 KJV). For many years, we heard this verse meant women were not allowed to wear pants because they were a man's garment. This caused much confusion in the church. Many women wore skirts and dresses as they worked in the garden and even when they went skating. Some were literally afraid of going to hell if they wore pants. Now, let's be realistic. Do you really think God would send someone to hell for wearing pants but allow an imperfect man to become a leader in his church? I don't believe this is the message the Lord was sending to his church! Later, we discovered that the Bible wasn't wrong; our theology was.

We learned many other doctrines that we thought pertained to holiness, such as the often quoted verse in Psalm 1. I am sure you recall these significant words: "Blessed is the man that walketh not in the counsel of the ungodly, nor standeth in the way of sinners, nor sitteth in the seat of the scornful. But his delight is in the law of the LORD, and in his law doth he meditate day and night."

Based on this verse, we were told not go to the movies, because, "Blessed is the man that does not sit in the *seat* of the scornful." The problem with that theology was that "scorners" (i.e., "sinners") also sat in banks, clubs, restaurants … You get my point. We were just handed a collection of Scriptures taken completely out of context that promoted an unhealthy view of holiness. We thought holiness consisted of what we did not do rather than who we were in Christ. God says, "You shall be holy because I am holy." Is God holy because of what he does or does *not* do? No, God is holy because of his character and his nature. "For I *am* the LORD your God: ye shall therefore sanctify yourselves, and ye shall be holy; for I *am* holy: neither shall ye defile yourselves with any manner of creeping thing that creepeth upon the earth" (Lev. 11:44 KJV).

As we read the Scriptures, we find that God took a great deal of time teaching his people how to live and conduct themselves in the new land. When the children of Israel came out of Egypt, they were going into a new country full of idols. God knew the Israelites would be tempted to worship them, so they needed something that would demonstrate the difference between God and the gods of the pagan nations. That difference was in the holy lives the children of Israel lived in contrast to the pagans. In short, the children of Israel were to be like God. Leviticus contains many verses that speak of the conduct, attitudes, and even the dietary laws the Israelites were to follow. Why did the Lord devote so much time to these instructions? The answer lies in the book of Ezekiel: "And they shall teach my people *the difference* between the holy and profane, and cause them to discern between the unclean and the clean" (Ezek. 44:23 KJV).

When I was a young recruit in the US Marine Corps, one of the greatest lessons I learned was that marines are different. We cut our hair differently and wore our uniforms differently from the other branches of service. We did this to set us apart and to indicate that we were an elite fighting force—ready to go further, strive harder, and do better than our peers. This attitude is reflected in the marines' slogan: "The few, the proud, the Marines." This indicates the type of people the Israelites were to be. They were no better than the surrounding people, merely set apart for service.

Do you recall what our parents said to us when we would behave in a manner that was contrary to our training? We tried to justify our behavior by saying, "Well, I only did it because everybody is doing it."

I'll bet your parents would say something like, "Well, if they jumped off of a bridge, would you do that too?" What they were actually saying was, "You should be different from others and learn to think for yourself." This is what the Lord is saying to us. We should strive to be different. Why? Because we are Christians. We represent the Lord Jesus, whose ways are truly superior to the ways of this world! Now do you understand why I called this chapter "The Challenge"? It is a challenge to live in the culture yet live separately as true saints of God. We must move beyond the limitations of the culture and learn to walk in the Spirit. A challenge indeed!

When I became a born-again believer in Christ, I had to make tremendous adjustments to my thinking process. Having spent a considerable amount of time in a church setting, my idea of being a Christian consisted of a list of things to do and things not allowed. I had no idea the Lord wanted a relationship with me. I could not comprehend that fact. God wanted to connect with me—period. The holiness he desired did not consist of what I did for him but who I was to him. Praise the Lord! When I finally discovered the reality of holiness, I began to enjoy my walk with Christ. Even so, the change to my lifestyle took time and effort. It was important to learn who I was in Christ. This was a difficult task, and I am thankful I had a pastor who taught me more about walking with God than doing things for God. Pastor Benjamin Smith was a very godly man, who I truly admire. In the realm of the Spirit, I wanted to be just like him.

One of Pastor Smith's favorite sayings was, "Let the Lord do something to you before doing something through you." It became apparent that this was essential as I watched, with great amazement, how people would boast about the Lord using them, even though they had no substance. They just could not live the life God required because they were trying to do it on their own. This behavior reminds me of the person Jesus spoke of in the Gospels: "Those on the rock are the ones who receive the word with joy when they hear it, but they have no root. They believe for a while, but in the time of testing they fall away" (Luke 8:13 NIV). I began to see the wisdom in my pastor's words. It was absolutely essential to surrender everything I was to the Lord so I could remain in him. I did not want to be a surface Christian; I wanted to be different. However, this was only the beginning of my journey into the teaching of biblical holiness.

As we saw in the previous chapter, Paul encourages us to avoid the trappings of the culture and be transformed by the renewing of our minds. I love this verse more each day because it provides the goal every Christian should desire to reach. My view is that holiness is, in short, godliness. That's right! It's about learning to live our lives in the spirit of God. We are to think as he would and obey the instructions he gave to the church while we live in this present world. Now we are going to have a real problem. How can a human be like God? While we can never be like God in a literal sense, we can certainly develop his attitude and views toward life.

Reading the Bible is one way to do this. As we fill our minds with his Word, our thought processes become godlier, as do our actions and reactions. By way of example, sometimes my wife of many years comments that we tend to finish each other's sentences as if we share the same mind. This comes from years of living together and learning to function as a team. This is the same principle that takes place in our relationship with the Lord. The more time we spend with him through prayer and reading his Word, the more we will sense his leading and direction. Connecting our minds to God's mind is crucial to separating from the culture and embarking down the path of holiness.

When I was a boy, my mother had some special dishes in the china closet in the dining room that we used only when we had guests. Even though those dishes were used only for special occasions, this did not prevent us from washing them and keeping them looking great. One time I asked why we had to wash the dishes if no one used them. My mother said we kept them clean in case we had company. Sounds funny, doesn't it? What if we put that concept into the realm of the things of God? Holiness is the practice of staying clean so you're ready when the Lord calls you into service and fellowship. Does it make more sense now?

When God came down to talk to Adam, the Scriptures say he came in the cool of the day. Many focus on the timing and give a myriad of reasons why the Lord would come at that particular time. However, I like to concentrate on the fact that he came down in the first place and that he did so without warning. Sometimes God just shows up, and if we walk in holiness, we will be prepared to meet him at any time. The focal point of holiness is obedience. As we walk in obedience, we experience the thrill of God's fellowship. God is good and loving, and he delights in his children. Proverbs 11:20 tells us, "They that are of a forward heart *are* abomination to the LORD: but *such as are* upright in *their* way *are* his delight." God calls us to walk upright and has promised to bless us when we comply with his word. Psalm 84:11 (NIV) reinforces this notion: "For the LORD God is a sun and shield; the LORD bestows favor and honor; no good thing does he withhold from those whose walk is blameless." Read that verse again. It tells us that the Lord will not withhold good things from those who walk with him with a clean life. This is directly related to a life of holiness and obedience. The discipline of holiness is the hallmark of Christianity, and it is what separates Christianity from mere religion. Holiness is a result of the connection with a holy God. It is not designed to produce a denomination or a system of doctrines. Holiness is what happens when we submit ourselves to the Lord Jesus and the Holy Spirit lives in our hearts. When we practice holiness, we don't just come to church; we become the church. Holiness positions us to be filled with the knowledge of the Lord and walk in his principles.

Today, we always hear that we are entitled to certain blessings simply by association. Yet the above text reveals something to the contrary. We must walk upright before him. The Lord is speaking of our walk of holiness. The challenge for you today is to resist the trappings of the culture and live in holiness before the Lord (Phil. 3:20 NIV). For some, that challenge means avoiding video games and movies that promote violence and hate. Others may be challenged to prevent the consumption of certain foods that harm the body. James teaches us to be aware of our lives and the decisions we make as children of God. "Anyone, then, who knows the good he ought to do and doesn't do it, sins" (James 4:17 NIV). We need the strength to live holy lives and remember we are citizens of heaven.

I love the words of the apostle Paul to the Philippian believers. He reminds them of their true citizenship: "but our citizenship is in heaven. And we eagerly await a Savior from there, the Lord Jesus Christ" (Phil. 3:20 NIV). When Paul says, "our citizenship is in heaven," I believe he was telling us that our thinking must reflect our new life. We must stop trying to fit in with this culture and face the reality that we do not belong here. We are pilgrims and strangers in this world, and we must learn the principles of a new society. As Hebrews 11:13 states, "These all died in faith, not having received the promises, but having seen them afar off, and were persuaded of *them,* and embraced *them,* and confessed that they were strangers and pilgrims on the earth." This reference teaches us that we are not to view this world as our home. We are simply travelers living amongst those who are not walking in the light of God's presence.

I love to travel. One of my favorite places to visit is Walt Disney World Resort in Orlando. I look forward to each trip with great anticipation, even as I book the hotel and make plane reservations. Usually, I cannot sleep well the night before, because I'm so excited. On the morning of the trip, a unique feeling of joy is resident in me as I focus on the journey. Are my bags packed? Do I have the plane tickets? Do I have traveler's checks and everything else I need? Does my family have everything they require as well? What does the weather hold in store for us?

After I arrive, I usually experience a feeling of relief as we pick up the rental car. The journey to the Disney property is about forty minutes from the airport (for me, that is!). As we pull up to the hotel, I feel another surge of joy and relief. We have finally arrived. All of our careful planning has paid off.

For the next several days, Disney World is our focal point. Then, about five days in, a new feeling develops as I begin thinking about the return home. By day seven, thoughts of home dominate my mind. Why do I feel this way? As much as I like Disney World, I do not live there. All of my family and friends are up north, and frankly, I get tired of living out of a suitcase. The truth is that I am merely a traveler and a stranger there. This is the way of Christians as we realize we are only pilgrims and strangers in this world. As much as we enjoy the world in which we live, eventually we realize we do not belong here and start preparing our minds to head home.

This is the challenge we face. We are in the world yet not of the world. We have been separated from the Lord and called to give him glory. We are to think as members of a new society, even as we live in the old. Holiness is the result of that discovery. God is holy, and he demands this of his children. We dare not allow the culture to distract us from our primary discipline of holiness. Regardless of what this postmodern world says, being godly (holy) is still the right thing to do.

We must not allow ourselves to become ensnared by this culture. Remember the words of the Scripture that teach us to, "Follow peace with all *men,* and holiness, without which no man shall see the Lord" (Heb. 12:14 KJV). Without holiness, no one can see the Lord. We must determine to live holy lives before our God and surrender ourselves into his hands. He is the only one who can keep us from falling into the traps set by the world. Let's determine to practice the discipline of living holy and enjoy the benefits of that life.

Let us pray:

Holy Father, I ask that you help me to live a holy life. I do not want to be swallowed up in the things of this culture. Grant me the peace and the strength to make the changes in my life that will please you. I ask this in Jesus's name. Amen.

Review questions:

1. Define holiness in your own words.
2. Is holiness a problem for you? Why?
3. Does the thought of practicing holiness bring you joy or sorrow?
4. What steps can you take to live a holy life? What habits do you need to break? What new attitudes or habits do you need to develop?

CHAPTER 3

The Conversion

Rather, clothe yourselves with the Lord Jesus Christ, and
do not think about how to gratify the desires of the sinful
nature. (Rom. 13:14 NIV)

SAMSON STRUGGLED WITH HIS FLESHLY desires. He had a habit of courting
the Philistine women. I guess the women of Israel were not as attractive,
or maybe they just reminded him of his duties as a judge. Either way, he
was so turned on by these Philistine women that he would visit them and
spend his passion on the very women whose lifestyles were opposite to that
which God had called him. Yes, Samson was headed for trouble. We all
know how the story ends. Samson allowed his fleshly desires to override his
calling as a judge. His life ended as a great tragedy yet a very real testimony
of what happens when we do not control the flesh.

Let's face it; we are called to lose our identity and become
representatives of Jesus in this present world. I am convinced that all
we do must reflect the life of Christ and draw people to the light of
the world—Jesus Christ. I know this seems difficult, but making this
adjustment is necessary if we want the world to see an apparent difference
between the things of God and the things of the fleshly world. When you

became a new creature in Christ, you receive a new life. For this life to have meaning, you must surrender to the lordship of Christ. I know this sounds a bit strange for those of us in the West because we fear God's commands will take away our pleasures. Yet, we cannot be like the world. It is not enough to be a believer; we must be converted. I tell people I do not preach for salvation; I preach for conversion. As the church devolves into another religion, many preachers feel satisfied when their sanctuary is filled with people. It seems like we are just preaching to fill a building. In fact, I have seen full buildings but no substantive change in the lives of the people there.

In the New Testament, the word often translated *converted* (from the Greek word *epistrepho*, ep-ee-stref'-o) carries the idea of "turning around, to turn." Often, we preach that people need to confess Christ, but there is no conversion, no turning. What good is it if we just come to the altar but continue to live the same way afterward? The actual test of Christianity is a changing of the heart. Conversion is the real work of Christ.

When I was a boy, I was quite a rebel at school. My behavior was not the best representation of my parents. I had two levels of behavior: one for school and the other for home. I did my best to ensure these two "hearts" never collided. Whenever the "bad heart" came forth, I received unwanted attention from my parents, and I would promise them I would not behave in that fashion again. Of course, there was sorrow and temporary repentance, yet there was no conversion. One incident, in particular, helps illustrate what happens when repentance is not followed by true conversion.

In grade seven, I had a peculiar problem with my math teacher, and I tormented this poor woman every chance I got. After trying to calm me down the normal way, she realized she needed help and threatened to call my parents. Panic rose inside. There was no way my parents could learn of my sin. I had to take steps to cover it up. So I did what any other normal child would do: I hurried home so I could answer the phone before my parents could.

When no call came in the evening, I was relieved. I figured that maybe my teacher had forgotten about me or was just trying to scare me. Either way, I was not going to take any chances. After my mom had gone to bed, I took the phone off the hook and then put it back in the cradle at around

11:00 p.m. I thought that my teacher would not call at such a late hour. In my mind, I had won. Still, I did not sleep well that night. Right before I finally dozed off, I remember thinking I was going to change (go to the altar). I was sorry and scared (repentance). I just wanted another chance, vowing my teacher wasn't going to have any more trouble with me (grace).

However, something happened that I did not count on. My math teacher called the house very early in the morning. I mean, what teacher calls before the sun comes up? Come on now; that was against the rules, never mind common courtesy! All of my plans failed, and my sin was exposed. Not only did she tell my mother about my behavior, but she also complained about not being able to reach anyone at our home the previous evening.

My parents' response was … Let's just say that if there were a department of human services in those days, I would have been removed from the home! However, their response changed my behavior not only toward that particular teacher but also toward school in general. In other words, I was converted. This is exactly what the Lord desires. The verses below help illustrate my point.

> For there is nothing covered, that shall not be revealed; neither hid, that shall not be known. (Luke 12:2 KJV)

> Wherewith shall I come before the LORD, *and* bow myself before the high God? Shall I come before him with burnt offerings, with calves of a year old? Will the LORD be pleased with thousands of rams, *or* with ten thousands of rivers of oil? Shall I give my firstborn *for* my transgression, the fruit of my body *for* the sin of my soul? He hath shewed thee, O man, what *is* good; and what doth the LORD require of thee, but to do justly, and to love mercy, and to walk humbly with thy God? (Mic. 6:6–8)

The Gospel of Luke says our sins will be exposed. This includes anything that is not washed by the precious blood of the Lamb. Just as I could not hide my behavior in school from my parents, no one can hide sins from God forever. At some point, there will be a reckoning! The culture is so full of temptations that we often find our lives full of hidden sins. Instead of seeking the Lord for forgiveness, we attempt to justify our behavior. We need to repent of the things that violate the law of God and are in direct disobedience to his revealed will. We have nothing to fear when we do because the Bible tells us the true nature of God is forgiveness and mercy.

The prophet Micah reveals the true heart of God. No more burnt offerings or acts of religious repentance. God does not want religious service; he wants conversion. For us to resist the culture, we must have a new power generator inside. We cannot be religious and defeat the cultural trappings of the world. The old attitudes of simply going to church on Sunday and Wednesday must be replaced by a new awareness of God's eternal presence. We must be mindful that the Lord is with us at every minute of every day. But this is a new day, and the Enemy is redirecting his attack. He has abandoned his goal of keeping us out of the church. He has also stopped trying to keep Christians from church work and doing things for the Lord. Instead, Satan has joined the church, entered the pulpit, and caused the Body of Christ to become just like the world. In case you doubt me, ask yourself this question: How many messages do you hear on the subject of conversion today? Most of our messages are about fluffy stuff that does not impress the Lord. We ministers must accept responsibility for the fact we have turned Christianity into a community of worldliness and fleshly demonstrations.

In the book of Acts, we find the very first use of the word *Christian*: "And when he had found him, he brought him unto Antioch. And it came to pass, that a whole year they assembled themselves with the church and taught much people. And the disciples were called Christians first in Antioch" (Acts 11:26 KJV). History tells us the name *Christian* was used initially as an insult, similar to how the term *Holy Roller* is used today. However, eventually to be called a follower of Christ became a badge of honor. To restore honor to this name today, Christians need to take some necessary steps, which are found in 1 Peter 2:1–3 (KJV): "Wherefore laying aside all malice, and all guile, and hypocrisies, and envies, and all evil speaking. As newborn babes, desire the sincere milk of the word that ye may grow thereby: If so be ye have tasted that the Lord is gracious." This is one of my favorite verses and a good place to begin our conversion process. Peter tells new believers that they must do certain things in light of their new birth in Christ. I especially like the order of the process. Let's unpack it.

1. We must abandon the characteristics of the old life. This verse contains an active indicator. It tells us to lay aside the things that cause us to miss out on a fellowship with the Lord. Often, I wonder how I can get closer to a holy God and live in a way that pleases him. Peter answers this question by saying we must lay aside the things that separate us from God. This is something we must do for ourselves. We cannot ask the Lord to do the things he has given us the power to perform. We must take the first step toward the goal of conversion. We must strip away all manner of lies, envy, wrath, and hypocrisy. We accomplish this by the decision to remove those things that are injurious to walking with the Lord. Peter says that we must divorce ourselves from every manner of behavior that results in extinguishing our lights. We *must* begin the process of sanctification and stick with it until there is a definitive change in habits and desires. This is a clear indication of our progress toward conversion. By deciding to change, we are well on our way to becoming like Jesus.

2. We must desire the sincere milk of the Word. The word *desire* (*epipotheō*) means "to long for." When was the last time you longed for the Word of God? When did you last want to stay in the Scriptures until your soul was satisfied? We should desire the Word of the Lord daily. Desiring something causes us to go after it with whole hearts.

When I was a young boy, my mother would make sweet potato pies. I'm telling you, they were some kind of good! When the pies were in the oven, our hearts—and stomachs—swelled with anticipation as we smelled the tasty ingredients. When they were ready to eat, there was great joy in the kitchen. I recall my desire to eat those pies vividly. It overrode any obstacle I may have encountered. This is how we should approach the Word of God, with hunger and the anticipation of being filled.

This is a critical issue for the believer today. Our goals have changed, and much of the preaching and teaching on the Bible does not build a desire for Christ in us. Much of what we hear is simply motivational speaking. Preachers talk about money, blessings, and comfortable lives that do not glorify God. It reminds me of the parable of the sower. "And some fell on stony ground, where it had not much earth; and immediately it sprang up, because it had no depth of earth: But when the sun was up, it was scorched; and because it had no root, it withered away" (Mark 4:5–6 KJV). Many believers hear the Word of God, yet they do not allow it to get deep into their hearts and minds and bring about change. The Word of God will not only bring change, but it will also remove those areas that do not glorify Christ. So let's study the Word of God and develop a hunger for the things of the Lord. As David said, "Thy Word have I hid in my heart that I might not sin against thee" (Psalm 119:11). After we employ these two most important steps, we must move to the next phase of the conversion process.

3. We must fellowship with other believers. Have you ever heard the phrase, "birds of a feather flock together?" We are all aware of the results of associating with people who are motivated to do something great with their lives. When we connect ourselves with winners, we adopt the same mind-set. Once we are converted to Christianity, our thought process needs to undergo a transformation. This happens when we begin to remove ourselves from those whose lives are contrary to Christ. You may think this is impossible, but with God, all things are possible. The passage below illustrates the importance of staying away from those who do not strive to be Christlike.

> Be ye not unequally yoked together with unbelievers: for what fellowship hath righteousness with unrighteousness? And what communion hath light with darkness? And what concord hath Christ with Belial? Or what part hath he that believeth with an infidel? And what agreement hath the temple of God with idols? For ye are the temple of the living God; as God hath said, I will dwell in them, and walk in *them;* and I will be their God, and they shall be my people. Wherefore come out from among them, and be ye separate, saith the Lord, and touch not the unclean *thing;* and I will receive you. (2 Cor. 6:14–17 KJV).

The church at Corinth had some serious problems, and the apostle Paul was frustrated with their behavior. This church was undisciplined and found it easy to fall back into worldly practices. Its people were unable to follow

Christian disciplines because of their unwillingness to live separate from the world. If we are to be effective for the Lord, we must disconnect ourselves from the trappings of the world and join ourselves with the people of God.

When I was a youth, I played baseball for the Oak Lane Youth Association. Boy, those were the good old days! Our team was called the Cougars. I was a pitcher, and the pressure to strike out our opponents was great. I can't tell you how relieved I was whenever the team cheered for me. It always lifted the weight. "Come on, Eric, you can do it. Strike the bum out!" The camaraderie provided the ability to play hard and win.

Today's Christians have undervalued the power of fellowship. When the apostle Paul told the Corinthians to live separately from the world, he wasn't trying to bring the church down; he was cheering them on! Living independently from the world leads us to a place of intimacy with God and each other. This type of biblical fellowship enables us to grow in the power of the Lord by sharing our gifts and abilities with each other. Proverbs 27:17 teaches us this valuable lesson: "Iron sharpeneth iron; so a man sharpeneth the countenance of his friend." If we are to rise above the mediocrity of the world, we must realize the value of fellowship. Don't take church services and Bible studies for granted. We must join with other believers and form valuable relationships that will strengthen us in the years to come.

Let us pray:

Father, please help me move closer toward the blessing of conversion. I desire to be all you need me to be in this dark world. Help me grow and develop into the person you created me to be. I pray that the Holy Spirit will enlighten me to the truth of your Word. I ask this in Jesus's name. Amen.

Review questions:

1. What are some behaviors that you need to put off?
2. What things snatch the Word of God from your heart?
3. What does Satan use to take your focus away from the Lord?
4. How can you overcome the Enemy's temptations and traps?

CHAPTER 4

Confronting the Enemy

Finally, be strong in the Lord and in his mighty power.
Put on the full armor of God so that you can take your
stand against the devil's schemes. For our struggle is not
against flesh and blood, but against the rulers, against
the authorities, against the powers of this dark world and
against the spiritual forces of evil in the heavenly realms.
(Eph. 6:10–12 NIV)

"IF ANYONE HITS YOU, YOU'D better hit back." These were the words of
instruction given to me as a child as I prepared to go to school. With this
advice planted firmly in my mind, I approached school with confidence,
believing I would be able to negotiate the rigors of academic life and thrive.
However, unknown to me, every other parent had told their children the
same thing. So I had to learn to confront some bullies who wanted to
demonstrate their abilities to beat up smaller children. The only way I
could survive was not to fight but to make friends. Making friends meant
I was going to have enemies. Someone was always looking to hurt others
when they were alone. This was the way of the world, and I had to learn
it fast. I thank God for my older brother, Garry. He would rough me up

sometimes so I understood what it took to defend myself. Garry taught me how to identify my enemies and how to stand up and be effective in life.

When you became a Christian, you were probably like me on my first day of school. You were so happy about your new life that you did not even think about your Enemy. Then you became aware of Satan, and other believers taught you how to defeat him and keep him at bay. While Satan is our primary enemy, as we search God's Word, we find that we are also at war with another power. "Love not the world," John's epistle teaches us. Like Satan, the worldly system is a Christian's other primary enemy, and we are advised to resist it as well.

Living the life to which God has called us puts us under enormous pressure. Paul warns us to be mindful, "lest Satan should get an advantage of us: for we are not ignorant of his devices" (2 Cor. 2:11). Despite this truth, most Christians spend their time resting and relaxing rather than engaging in battle. History has proven that the greatest generals were students of warfare. In contrast, we are often at a disadvantage because we are unaware of how to wage war with the Enemy of our souls. We have lost our fighting edge. When the apostle Paul spoke of the Enemy's *devices*, he used the Greek word *noema*. This word carries the idea of a perception, or thoughts and purpose. Paul is telling us we need to understand our Enemy's purpose and ability. This is where we usually lose the battle. We underestimate Satan and, as a result, find ourselves struggling with his devices. Every battle has a plan, and every adversary has a purpose. Usually, we see the conflict, but we do not always see the purpose. If we understand the Enemy's purpose, we will be more than able to stand against his schemes.

In John 10:10, Jesus reveals the true heart of the Enemy. He is a thief who comes to steal, kill, and destroy. This is the most concise identification of the Enemy's purpose. He has come to bring destruction so that God's children will focus on the damage he causes rather than live for the Lord.

During my early days as a Christian, our pastor spent much time teaching us how to resist Satan's devices and live as Christians in a world that was clearly anti-Christ. I can boil all of his teachings down to one simple saying: "Touch not, taste not, and handle not." We were simply to avoid anything that had Satan's smell attached to it. So we avoided movie theaters and anything considered worldly. We focused on the major sins and left the smaller sins alone. I am convinced our Enemy quietly observed our desire to live for the Lord and then formulated a new plan of action.

I watched with amazement when sin went from the public eye to the subtlety of the private life. With the advent of electronic media, it became easier to commit certain sins as the tools of satan had changed. I believe satan thought, "If I can't get Christians to come to me, I will go to them." Our lives were changed when we were able to sin in private and indulge our desires in the comfort of our homes so that no one would know. As the battle plan unfolded, Christians were not prepared for the assault. Just as America was not ready for 9/11, we were not looking for the attack on the home front. We kept looking for some ominous cloud of demonic activity to fight against. Yet our adversary hit us where we were not looking.

Satan's greatest desire is to weaken God's children through worldly lusts and bring dishonor to our Lord and frustrate the purpose of Christ. Throughout history, we have seen this struggle play out on many fronts. Satan fights against the true worship of God, and then he attacks the government, world economies, and even our bodies. In times past, he would usually find the church engaged in worship and getting closer to the Lord. However, in these last few decades, Satan has found the church weak and full of fleshly desires and thoughts that weaken the power of God in the lives of the people.

I believe our adversary considered what was important to the Lord and decided to strike out at that very thing. He (Satan) may have pondered, what has always been the apple of God's eye? What has always been an outstanding example of the Lord to use in the world? What would demonstrate His love for humanity? The answer undoubtedly came to him with clarity: families are important to God. So Satan decided to destroy the family to bring down the church.

The church has always been a community of believers made up of well-ordered families. Through the family, the church would flourish. Since the 1960s, however, the family has been in decline in America. I suspect there are some reasons for this decrease. After World War II, our nation saw a shortage of men in the home. Women had to take a more active role in the leadership of the home. As a result, the structure of the traditional two-parent family changed. When our nation entered the Korean conflict, we found ourselves again with an absence of men (and women) in the home, and the traditional family suffered once more. When our troops finally returned home, the country was radically different, and there was no turning back to the traditional views we once held so dear. As we moved toward more single-parent homes, we saw the removal of discipline and biblical examples of godliness. With the absence of strong male leadership, it became evident that our children were going to be at a disadvantage.

Having seen the results of single-parent homes, I can say that women have done a fabulous job with the new role thrust upon them. So don't get me wrong. Women are fully capable of building strong, healthy families. However, I do believe their position is much easier if there is a godly man in the home to provide essential leadership to give our children what they need to be productive. Our Enemy has taken advantage of the breakdown of the family to bring destruction to our culture. When there are no guidelines at home, our children fall for the devices that are presented to them in the world.

When I was a child, my brother and I had to shovel coal into the heater, and it was our responsibility to ensure the burner did not go out. Part of my duties (being the younger child) was to remove the ashes. My brother and I took those responsibilities seriously because we knew there would be grave consequences if we did not. The discipline our father instilled in us for a seemingly trivial detail gave both of us a sound work ethic. It also taught us to honor our father and obey his instructions, even when he was not home.

When the Lord tells us to stay away from the trappings of the world, our Father is giving us instructions that we must obey him every day. God's command is clear to all of his children: "Do not love the world, not the things of the world." If we look at the worldly culture, we find that the Scriptures are right. The world is made up of the pride of life, the lust of the eye, and the lust of the flesh.

We must recognize these traps and avoid being caught up in them. Let's examine each one in turn.

The Pride of Life

> In his arrogance, the wicked man hunts down the weak, who are caught in the schemes he devises. He boasts of the cravings of his heart; he blesses the greedy and reviles the LORD. In his pride the wicked does not seek him; in all his thoughts there is no room for God. his ways are always prosperous; he is haughty and your laws are far from him; he sneers at all his enemies. He says to himself, "Nothing will shake me; I'll always be happy and never have trouble. His mouth is full of curses and lies and threats; trouble and evil are under his tongue. (Psalm 10:2–7 NIV)

The pride of life speaks to the arrogance and the need for self-importance. In the psalm quoted above, we see the development of what I like to call "the man of ego." He takes a position that is contrary to the Lord. In fact, he avoids the Lord altogether. Does this attitude sound familiar? Our country is filled with arrogance. We move forward without ever acknowledging the Lord, who has kept us. In fact, on many occasions, our country was spared certain disaster, and then the people took a cavalier attitude toward the Lord and his grace. This was best typified by the September 11, 2001, terrorist attacks. America had not experienced a disaster of this magnitude since the surprise attack on Pearl Harbor. After holding their breath in fear for a few days, most people went back to business as usual. I suspect that the church responded in a fashion that was exemplified by the world. We did not call our congregations to prayer (for the most part), nor did we redirect our focus and seek the Lord with intensity. We passed up a golden opportunity to convene prayer sessions that reflected God's grace. We serve a God, who responds to repentance and humility. Therefore, we must view tragedy as a call from the Lord to spend more time with him. He calls us into a season of prayer as never before. Pride keeps us from talking to God, but pride goes before destruction.

One of my mentors, the late Pastor Raymond Baylor of Bibleway Evangelistic Church, often told me, "Those who will talk to men about God must first talk to God about men." It is the height of arrogance to stand before the Lord's people and think you can speak for God if you have not spent time with him. As we move into the next season of the Lord's work, I pray that we will develop attitudes of humility. Here is a story from the Word of the Lord that clearly illustrates my point concerning arrogance.

> At the end of twelve months, he walked in the palace of the kingdom of Babylon.
>
> The king spake, and said, Is not this great Babylon, that I have built for the house of the kingdom by the might of my power, and for the honour of my majesty? While the word *was* in the king's mouth, there fell a voice from heaven, *saying,* O king Nebuchadnezzar, to thee it is spoken; The kingdom is departed from thee. And they shall drive thee from men, and thy dwelling *shall be* with the beasts of the field: they shall make thee to eat grass as oxen, and seven times shall pass over thee, until thou know that the most High ruleth in the kingdom of men, and giveth it to whomsoever he will. The same hour was the thing fulfilled upon Nebuchadnezzar: and he was driven from men, and did eat grass as oxen, and his body was wet with the dew of heaven, till his hairs were grown like eagles' *feathers,* and his nails like birds' *claws.* (Dan. 4:28–33 KJV)

King Nebuchadnezzar actually thought the greatness of his kingdom was due to his efforts. Can you imagine the arrogance of this man? Verses 31–33 tell us that the Lord gave Nebuchadnezzar a quick lesson in humility! Just think about it, being in your palatial home one moment and then finding yourself in the fields eating like an animal the next. Talk about a fast track to humility! Now, let's see Nebuchadnezzar's response.

> And at the end of the days I Nebuchadnezzar lifted up mine eyes unto heaven, and mine understanding returned unto me, and I blessed the most High, and I praised and

honoured him that liveth for ever, whose dominion *is* an everlasting dominion, and his kingdom *is* from generation to generation: And all the inhabitants of the earth *are* reputed as nothing: and he doeth according to his will in the army of heaven, and *among* the inhabitants of the earth: and none can stay his hand, or say unto him, What doest thou? At the same time my reason returned unto me; and for the glory of my kingdom, mine honour and brightness returned unto me; and my counsellors and my lords sought unto me; and I was established in my kingdom, and excellent majesty was added unto me. Now I Nebuchadnezzar praise and extol and honour the King of heaven, all whose works *are* truth, and his ways judgment: and those that walk in pride he is able to abase. (Dan. 4:34–37 KJV)

My favorite verse is verse 37 when Nebuchadnezzar states that he will honor the King of Heaven, and God says those who walk in pride will be brought low. This is why the apostle John tells us pride separates us from the Father. I urge you to remember that your possessions come from God's merciful hand. Never forget his grace. Hear the words of the apostle Paul in 1 Corinthians 4:7 (NIV): "For who makes you different from anyone else? What do you have that you did not receive? And if you did receive it, why do you boast as though you did not? What do you have that you did not receive?" We can do nothing on our own. All of us are the recipients of God's unfathomable mercy and grace. In light of that fact, there is no room for pride or arrogance. Be humble before the Lord, and he will exalt you in due time.

Lust of the Eye

The next area John addresses is the lust of the eye. This is a very real problem for the average believer. It speaks to the sin of covetousness, and covetousness is greed. Greed only means that you want what you see. In America, we place a lot of emphasis on materialistic wealth. We want people to see our prosperity and remark on how the Lord is blessing us. We must be careful about this attitude lest we fall into the Enemy's trap.

Have you ever taken a drive through an affluent neighborhood just to look at the houses? Be honest; while you were looking at those fabulous homes, didn't you feel like God should give you one of those mansions like you *deserved*? Did you notice that when you returned home, you began to find problems with your house, giving you all the more reason to move into your "blessing"? This feeling of uneasiness originates in the lust of the eye. You saw something you wanted, and you began to claim it by faith. The scriptural teaching of contentment went right out the window. Jesus was too smart to fall for the lust of the eye. When Satan approached him regarding the kingdoms of this world, Jesus refused to be bribed, as recounted in Matthew 4:8–10 (NIV).

> Again, Satan took him to a very high mountain and showed him all the kingdoms of the world and their splendor. "All this I will give you," he said, "if you will bow down and worship me." Jesus said to him, "Away from me, Satan! For it is written: 'Worship the Lord your God, and serve him only.'"

Jesus realized Satan's bribe had some serious strings attached. If Jesus accepted it, he would have to bow down and worship Satan. Wow! Christ's response speaks volumes to us today. When the lust of the eye leads us astray, it can lead us to bow down to Satan. What a revelation! Think about this: You see that beautiful house or that luxury car, and you determine you must have it. Yet your income does not support your desire. Well, guess what? You take on a second job, and where will that time come from? You guessed it, your time with the Lord. Then you discover you need some extra money for your new blessing. Guess where that money will come from. Right again! The Lord's work. Do you see where I am going with this? We see so much in the course of the day, and we want so much of what we see that we neglect to commune with our Heavenly Father. The Apostle Paul gives great encouragement to the church with these words, "Not that I speak in respect of want: for I have learned, in whatsoever state I am, *therewith* to be content" (Phil. 4:11 KJV). Have you learned to be content with the state the Lord has you in at this point in life? I am not saying we should not strive to better ourselves, but our pursuit of happiness should not blind us to reality.

Read this passage from Matthew 25:14–15 (KJV).

> For the kingdom of heaven is as a man traveling into a far country, who called his own servants, and delivered unto them his goods. And unto one he gave five talents, to another two, and to another one; to every man according to his several ability; and straightway took his journey.

Note the phrase, "according to his several ability." I believe the Lord will only make us responsible for what we can accomplish. There was never a time when I wanted to be a doctor. I just don't have that ability, and I think the Lord kept me from pursuing a dream that would have caused me frustration. Now, I did have the capacity to become a lawyer. I love debate and research and the thrill of helping people out of dilemmas. I would have loved being a lawyer! However, the Lord took my law skills and made me a pastor. Now, I represent the King of Kings, Jesus!

Here is my point: whenever we lose contentment with our gifts, calling, possessions, and position in life, we are liable to fall into the lust of the eye. We must keep our eyes on the Lord Jesus and not on the works or gifts that someone else possesses. I urge you to take control of your eyes. If the Enemy is successful in getting you to look at the things others possess, you will become frustrated and then fall into covetousness. Our culture breeds competition. We can also find this attitude in the church. I have been in ministerial meetings where the focus was on how many members each pastor has at his church. Then the conversation usually migrates toward different programs and activities designed to attract still more people. Many ministers are secretly competing for status and people, focusing on numbers instead of connecting with the Lord and helping others to do the same. The hope for unity is lost in the church today as we seek to build a better church than the "guy down the street." We have adopted the philosophy that bigger is better, even when it comes to the kingdom. We look at the so-called success of someone else and we desire the same things that they have. Soon, the obsession to be better takes over, and sin hatches.

Sadly, this happened once in my own ministry. Our church had just moved into a new building. The Lord allowed us to take ownership of an old appliance store, which required some major renovations. Shortly after we took possession of the building, we had an extraordinary service. The guest preacher had been an acquaintance of mine for some years. When he stood up to give his sermon, his first words were, "I want to thank the Lord for your new building. I am glad for you, and I do not have a jealous bone in my whole body."

That threw me for a loop! If he weren't jealous, he would not have said those words. "Oh well," I thought, "I guess we are in for a night of this person trying to show just how gifted he is." That's exactly what happened. Do you see how easy it is for the lust of the eye to take over? We live in an extremely visual world, which can be both positive and negative. Jesus says we can have what we say (Mark 11). When we think about our words (tools), they are created in the mind. Therefore, we are able to see what we want. Once that vision is clear in the spirit, we may see the thing in the natural. When we use our vision for positive things, we are able to see those things that are pleasing to the Lord. Jesus said that he only did what he saw his Father doing (John 5:19)!

When the Lord instructed me to plant Bethel, he literally showed me the church and what Bethel was to be and do. That was a shock to me, and I must tell you I was a bit taken aback by the size of the congregation. At the time, I was preaching on a regular basis, but we had not even started the ministry. Yet the Lord showed me the future of this church. We praise the Lord for his goodness, as the things I saw are still being fulfilled.

When Satan uses our visual gifts for his purposes, we often find ourselves in the arena of lust. He wants us to see something so that we begin to covet it and then create plans to get it. We must continue to tame our flesh and our eyes so we will remain above the lust that comes from vision and imagination.

Let's grow up and stop being governed by the lust of the eyes. Let's keep our eyes on Jesus instead. Rejoice with whatever the Lord has given to you. I am not better than anyone, and no one is better than me. We are all different, yet we complement each other in the work of the Lord. I pray that you will avoid the lust of the eyes and discover the joy of serving the Lord with your unique gifts.

Lust of the Flesh

> Let not sin therefore reign in your mortal body, that ye should obey it in the lusts thereof. Neither yield ye your members *as* instruments of unrighteousness unto sin: but yield yourselves unto God, as those that are alive from the dead, and your members *as* instruments of righteousness unto God. (Rom. 6:12–13 KJV)

Our culture is a breeding ground for the lust of the flesh. If there is a universal stronghold among believers, the lust of the flesh is it. Now, I do not want to oversimplify the term to mean merely sexual perversion. The lust of the flesh also speaks to individualism, that stubborn part of us that says, "Lord, I am going to do what I want to do, regardless of your words." In the above passage, the apostle Paul instructs us to take control of our flesh and yield our members to the Lord. I find it interesting that Paul refers to the flesh as though it were a person. He uses the words *reign, obey,* and *yield.* I'll bet you never thought of the flesh as something you would obey or yield to, did you? Simply put, the flesh can become our worst enemy. It wants what it wants, whenever it wants it. Whew! The desires of the flesh are all consuming, and we must do everything in our power to separate ourselves from the things that enslave the flesh. Each generation has produced its own flesh-gratifying actions, trapping us in the very actions our Lord warns us away from. Our culture today is no different.

When I became a Christian in 1971, the church was still teaching the so-called doctrines of holiness. Christians did not participate in many things that were doctrinally improper. While we were not sure there was a biblical precedent for the prohibition, we fell in line with the doctrines of the moment. It now appears that we were in a type of bondage. We were taught that our clothing was to exemplify Christ, and we were not to wear anything that could have been identified as lustful or lewd. Our mind-set of God was one of fear. He was not one to be played with or ignored, and if you did not respect him, there would be dire consequences.

I do agree that there is to be a qualitative difference between the church and the world. However, I am not so sure that difference is to be motivated out of fear and dread. This attitude was very prominent in the church until the end of the 1960s. Something took place as we approached the end of the decade that revolutionized the doctrines of holiness. We discovered the word *charismatic*. Now, what in the world did that word mean? I think the teachers of this doctrine were trying to extract something from the Greek word *charis*, which meant "acceptable, benefit, favor, gift, grace (-ious), joy, liberality, pleasure, thank (-s, -worthy)." I believe the idea was to remove the so-called "fear of God" and turn us into fun-loving, no-holds-barred hippie types. It caught on like wildfire. Suddenly, God was our friend, and we were to be friendly with our Creator. We developed a type of overfamiliarity for the Lord. In my opinion, this new attitude towards God may have sent an improper message. Some may have thought we could live undisciplined lives because the Lord was our friend, and we were going to be with him anyway.

Churches began to relax standards of holiness, and our lives were compromised. Seemingly overnight, there was no difference between the children of God and the children of Satan. It was a repeat of the situation between Balaam and Balak. When it became apparent to Balaam that he could not curse the children of Israel, he instructed King Balak to allow the Moabite women to run wild in the camp of the Israelites. When this compromise was reached, a curse came upon the children of God. They literally cursed themselves, as Numbers 31:14–16 (KJV) describes.

> Moses was wroth with the officers of the host, with the captains over thousands, and captains over hundreds, which came from the battle. And Moses said unto them, Have ye saved all the women alive? Behold, these caused the children of Israel, through the counsel of Balaam, to commit trespass against the LORD in the matter of Peor, and there was a plague among the congregation of the LORD.

Removing biblical standards of holiness has left us wide open to deception and false doctrines. The attitude of doing it "my way" has done nothing but cause trouble for the children of God.

My parents set boundaries for me and my siblings. These boundaries were not pleasant, but they were necessary for our survival and subsequent development. In the same way, we must have structure in our lives if we are to be successful. If we obey the flesh, we will be defeated every time. Paul tells us that the flesh is something to be disciplined. "Do not yield your members as instruments of unrighteousness." Do not yield! This phrase carries the idea that you have a choice. You can tell your flesh that you will not do what it wants. It's that simple.

Our culture provides many avenues of pleasure for the flesh. From the simplicity of television to the horror of Internet pornography, this culture not only provides ways for fleshly gratification, but it also removes our guilt. "Go ahead," the flesh says, "God understands, and he will forgive you." However, neither the flesh nor the culture tells you what happens to lives without discipline.

Satan's Battle Plan and the Defeat of Christians

> So Delilah said to Samson, Tell me the secret of your great strength and how you can be tied up and subdued. (Judg. 16:6 NIV)

Three times the Philistine woman begged Samson for his secret. Three times she lulled him into a false sense of security. Three times! You'd think Samson would wonder what was going on or at least think, "This woman is after my anointing, and I must get away from her." However, I suspect she smelled nice, spoke softly to him, and caressed him gently. These were the ingredients for the fall of a great man of God. Now, let's look at one of the saddest verses in the whole Bible in 31:14 (KJV): "Then she called, 'Samson, the Philistines are upon you!' He awoke from his sleep and thought, 'I'll go out as before and shake myself free.' But he did not know that the LORD had left him." The fact Samson did not know the Lord had left him is a sobering thought. Yet we can find ourselves in the same position. We can give in to Delilah (the world), submit to her passions (the flesh), and surrender the anointing, which is given for the service of the Lord. Yes, we will have momentary pleasures, but those moments may result in a loss of the unique ability to serve the Lord. So we must ask if the pleasure is worth the loss of anointing. Imagine wanting to work for the Lord and discovering that your spiritual strength has been removed by a moment of temporary passion. The lust of the flesh is a deadly tool that our Enemy loves to use. We Americans have become so lustful that the things we used to avoid (carnal talk, sexual immorality, and overindulgence) are now common among us. The world has more influence over the children of God today than ever before.

The book of Numbers tells us that after the Israelites had crossed the Red Sea, they were so blessed that other nations were afraid of them. In fact, Balak, the Moabite king, wanted the prophet Balaam to curse the people of God. However, the Lord directed Balaam to avoid conflict with his people. Even though the Israelites were blessed by God, they decided to enter into a lifestyle that was contrary to his will. The following passages tell us what happens when you leave your position of blessing and fall to the lust of the flesh:

> While Israel was staying in Shittim, the men began to indulge in sexual immorality with Moabite women, who invited them to the sacrifices to their gods. The people ate and bowed down before these gods. So Israel joined in worshiping the Baal of Peor. And the LORD's anger burned against them. (Num. 25:1–3 NIV)

If you live by fleshly desires, the Lord's anger will rest on your life. We need to fix this area of our lives and return to walking in holiness and avoiding the lust of the flesh. Here are some helpful steps.

Step 1: Return to the Lord with all your heart.

Step 2: Give up the fleshly desires and abandon fleshly lusts.

Step 3: Seek the Lord early and often.

Step 4: Identify the possible "Delilah" in your life, and do not submit to her charms.

Step 5: Saturate your mind and spirit with the Word of God. This is critical because the Word is the source of cleansing and strength. "Wherewithal shall a young man cleanse his way? By taking heed thereto according to thy word" (Psalm 119:9 KJV).

These radical actions will not come easy. Behaviors take the time to change, and when those behaviors are connected to our spirit being, we may find it a bit harder to change our habits. We must appeal to the Lord Jesus for the help we need to change. Just as a drug addict has to fight to be delivered, deliverance from lust and pride must also be taken seriously. The flesh will not just roll over and die. It will always remind you of the pleasurable times you had in your past. That's why you need the strength of the Lord Jesus to help you. When you make up your mind to be victorious, you will be.

Let us pray:

Father, please help me resist the power of my flesh and turn my life over to your hands. You have made me more than a conqueror, and I pledge to walk in that power. I ask you to cleanse my heart and mind and help me find that special place of holiness that pleases you. Jesus, take complete control of my life. I submit to your lordship and power. Thank you for hearing my prayer. Amen.

Review questions:

1. In which of the three areas discussed in this chapter are you most vulnerable to attacks from Satan?
2. What steps are you taking to reconnect to the Lord with all your heart?

CHAPTER 5

Escaping the Culture

If they have escaped the corruption of the world by knowing our Lord and Savior Jesus Christ and are again entangled in it and overcome, they are worse off at the end than they were at the beginning. (2 Peter 2:20 NIV)

PETER NOTED THAT SOME CHRISTIANS had successfully escaped the pollution of the world through their knowledge of Christ. However, these same Christians were overcome by the culture and were worse off than they were at their initial conversion. What do you think caused their demise? It appears that the Christians became entrapped by the culture that surrounded them and lost sight of Jesus.

Sadly, we are in the same position as they were. In fact, we are more deliberate in our backsliding just because we have become numb to the sins of our culture and lost the real intimacy we once had with the Lord. It is time we escape the traps and snares that the Enemy uses to bring us into spiritual mediocrity. I have watched the church lose its uniqueness and purpose. It appears that the body of Christ has become no more than a group of people looking for a place to fit into a world that is on a collision course with God's judgment. The Bible has been reduced to a book of cute euphemisms that guarantee the reader a life of wealth and luxury. Our churches have abandoned terms like *deliverance, holiness,* and *godliness.* We have replaced them with defeated phrases, such as, "I cannot live this life," "It's too hard," and "I just can't make it anymore." These phrases relieve us of an obligation to represent Jesus. It seems as though the culture has won, and all we can do is wait for the Lord to return. Is this really all that's left for us?

As I observe the body of Christ, I am saddened to see that the real essence of our relationship has seemingly died. What started as a dynamic relationship with the Lord Jesus became a culture-driven, lackluster attempt to use the Lord to build our own kingdoms. We are in a prison of sorts, and it is time to escape! It reminds me of this verse from Exodus 9:13 (KJV): "And the LORD said unto Moses, Rise up early in the morning, and stand before Pharaoh, and say unto him, Thus saith the LORD God of the Hebrews, Let my people go, that they may serve me." When the children of Israel were in Egypt, the Lord wanted them to leave that culture so they could serve him freely. In fact, seven verses in Exodus contain the phrase "Let my people go so they may serve me!" Like the Israelites, we leave the trappings of the culture and separate ourselves from the lifestyles of our past so we are free to serve God.

When the church was new, people had a strong desire to separate themselves from the world. They believed that sanctification—escaping the culture—was the key to living effectively for the Lord. We see this teaching throughout Paul's writings.

> Wherefore come out from among them, and be ye separate, saith the Lord, and touch not the unclean *thing;* and I will receive you. And will be a Father unto you, and ye shall be my sons and daughters, saith the Lord Almighty. Having therefore these promises, dearly beloved, let us cleanse ourselves from all filthiness of the flesh and spirit, perfecting holiness in the fear of God. (2 Cor. 6:17–7:1 KJV)

When we examine Paul's letters to the Corinthians, we find a unique link to today's church. This makes the church at Corinth a model for what happens to a church when it adjusts its doctrines to its surroundings rather than to the heart of God.

Paul visited the city in AD 51 or 52 and found the believers in a state of carnality. In fact, Paul tells us that he was a bit intimidated by them: "And I was with you in weakness, and in fear, and in much trembling" (1 Cor. 2:3 KJV). Paul saw a church on the verge of collapsing because of cultural influences. Among other things, he found the following:

- carnality
- immaturity
- fleshly demonstrations of spiritual gifts
- lack of love
- high divorce rates
- false apostles
- fighting for positions
- sexual perversion

Does this sound familiar as we examine the church today? I'll say it again: We must escape the trappings of our culture and shine as the true light that Christ says we are.

When the church became culturally driven, our standards of biblical holiness began to change. It appeared that the Bible was no longer the final authority on matters of our lives. It seemed that we just drifted into a more humanistic concept of life. I believe that we began to construct a view of God that was not supported by the Holy Bible. Suddenly it became easier to make God fit into our lives, rather than change ourselves to fit into his will. Now it appears that we endorse the very things we once rejected as demonic and ungodly. Do you recall the days when people had a healthy fear of the Lord? In those days, we exercised extreme care when we entered the house of worship. We dressed modestly, and we demanded that our preachers and teachers live what they taught. The Word of God was the absolute authority in our lives, and we dared not try to change its content. Now, the Bible has been watered down so much that many of God's children do not even believe it anymore. Rather than growing in their knowledge of God, many modern Christians seem to use new information to challenge the Word of God. One of the most prevalent questions I receive is about the Word's power. Is the Bible really the living Word? This issue goes to the core of our faith. If we doubt the Word, what do we have to stand on in times of distress? Remember that the first sin originated from the question, "Hath God said?" So the principle challenge for us today is to stand on the fact that the Word of God is truly powerful and able to help us in every area of life. The Holy Scriptures are designed to teach us how to live from the Lord's perspective, not ours. The Word is not to be debated, compromised, challenged, or enslaved by the culture. The Word of God must be obeyed, believed, quoted, and trusted. Unfortunately, we have moved into a new realm of doing what is right in our own eyes and ignoring the Word's teachings. We need to come out of the culture and get the culture out of us.

The things that hindered the Corinthian church are alive and well in the twenty-first century church. Things are deteriorating, and no one is speaking up for the Lord on a consistent basis. If we are not careful, we will begin to take on the character of the church at Corinth. There is so much competition between our preachers and leaders, and I believe that action grieves the Holy Spirit. There is an attitude that the anointing belongs to a person or a private group as opposed to the entire body of Christ. Leaders fight and compete over church members, desirous of vainglory, and then boast to say they have the largest congregations. By adopting the standards of this age, there is a conflict with the Word of the Lord, and some have even lowered their standards of Godliness to have more people join their individual congregations. Yes, it appears that we have become like Corinth, and we must escape! I believe that it is still possible for us to avoid the trappings of the world and come back to the feet of a loving Savior. He is still able to receive and heal those who come to him and request his help.

I can hear the Lord crying out to the world, "Let my people go!" However, we do need a Moses to stand and cry against the injustice of sin and bondage. The people of God are not hopeless, just temporarily off course. Jesus needs someone who is willing to lose everything to gain Christ. Who is ready to step up? Are you? As we watch the church sink deeper and deeper in the very culture that once enslaved us, we need to do everything in our power to return to the heart of God.

Now, Let's Escape!

> But our citizenship is in heaven. And we eagerly await a
> Savior from there, the Lord Jesus Christ. (Phil. 3:20 NIV)

In his letter to the Philippians, Paul teaches that we are to look for a Savior from heaven. The simple truth here is that we must shift our vision from the earth to heaven. We are citizens of heaven, so we must learn the principles of that kingdom. While we wait for Jesus, we must live for him and demonstrate his love, power, and presence. Jesus tells us to "seek the kingdom" and things will change for us. After researching the word *seek,* I think Jesus was telling us we must find out how the kingdom works. To be victorious in our Christian walks, we must learn the secrets of God's kingdom. We will only escape the trappings of this world when we focus on our true world, the Kingdom of God.

As I noted previously, the church is being bombarded with the sins of the flesh and the culture. Pride has replaced humility, and we actually think we can be successful without the anointing. We have undergone a significant paradigm shift. As we become more educated, we believe that the Lord is here to serve us. The very things that the Lord warned us about in his Holy Word have come true in our lifetime. Unfortunately, many Christians are powerless against the trappings of this culture and the attacks Satan brings against them. Therefore, we must overcome our spiritual ignorance and accept that we are incapable of standing against the Enemy without Christ.

I remember when there was a cry from our hearts just to sit with Jesus when we would sit in his divine presence and receive from the glow of his glory. I recall the days when there was a great hush as we waited for him and enjoyed his presence. Oh, how I long for those days of intimacy with the Lord again. I miss those times when his church would rejoice in him and not in what he could do for us. The season for such intimacy seems long past, but it can be recovered if we escape the culture.

Seek, Set, and Die!

> If ye then be risen with Christ, seek those things which
> are above, where Christ sitteth on the right hand of God.
> Set your affection on things above, not on things on the
> earth. For ye are dead, and your life is hid with Christ in
> God. (Col. 3:1–3 KJV)

When the apostle Paul wrote to the church at Colosse, he wanted
to free them from the trappings of their culture. He brought a sense of
liberty to an otherwise oppressed body of believers. Their oppression
was caused by the constant badgering of a group of legalistic teachers
who sought to exercise control over the new church at Colosse. This
control was the result of doctrinal teachings that were designed to
keep believers in ritualistic bondage, rather than helping them to find
fulfillment in their relationships with Christ. Paul encouraged these
believers to seek the Lord, set their affections on him, and die to the
world. If we hope to escape the culture, we must adopt this same
attitude.

The spirit world hates a vacuum, so if you have been born again, you
must fill your life with the things of God. Christian maturity does not
just happen; you have to work at it! Paul says we must move on after we
seek the Lord and set our affections on things above. I know this presents
a significant challenge to believers today because so many things demand
our time. Yet, we know the Lord would not call us to do anything he did
not equip us to do. "Set your affections" simply means that we should
redirect our thoughts to the things of God. He should occupy the majority
of our thoughts, and we must develop the art of bringing our ideas in line
with his. This takes discipline and effort, but I know we can do it through
Christ.

In my experience as a Christian, I have learned that controlling my
thought life is paramount to Christ being formed in me. This is one area
where we lack discipline. Paul admonished the believers in Philippi to
control their thoughts by allowing the mind of Christ to reign. I believe
Paul was also trying to drill into the Christians at Colosse. He sought to

give them a sense of liberty and encouraged them to focus on the new life in Christ as opposed to the foolishness of the culture.

> Since you died with Christ to the fundamental principles of this world, why, as though you still belonged to it, do you submit to its rules: "Do not handle! Do not taste! Do not touch!" And "These are all destined to perish with use, because they are based on human commands and teachings." (Col. 2:20–22 NIV)

Paul encouraged the believers to leave the things the culture generated and move on to the richness of a relationship with the Lord. We are still being bombarded with doctrines of legalism. Legalism seeks a level of control that may cause the church to abandon a positive relationship with the Lord. This will be the result of being driven by doctrine rather than being driven by a desire to connect with our Lord. Paul encouraged them to escape the culture and return to the Lord. He used a phrase he was so fond of whenever he explained the life believers were expected to live. In Colossians 3:9–10 (NIV), Paul tells men to "not lie to each other, since you have taken off your old self with its practices and have put on the new self, which is being renewed in knowledge in the image of its Creator." He also states in Ephesians 4:22–24 (NIV) that man was "taught, with regard to your former way of life, to put off your old self, which is being corrupted by its deceitful desires; to be made new in the attitude of your minds; and to put on the new self, created to be like God in true righteousness and holiness." In both of these references, Paul encourages us to put on the new self. The new self, or new man, as it is written in the King James Version, is the exact opposite of the culture. The new person is making the transition from the world of selfish pleasures, lust, and pride. We then go on to a new existence filled with the love of God and the ability to live above the sins of the flesh. Hallelujah!

When we master the connection between the new man and the new thought life, we will see substantial changes in our Christian walks. Remember the children of Israel and how the Lord wanted them out of Egypt? There was a very simple reason for the Lord's command. He wanted his children in a place where they could worship him without the encumbrances of the world. If this was true of the children of Israel, it is also true of God's children today. We must do the following to escape the culture.

- Seek the Lord.
- Set our affections on things above.
- Put on the new man.
- Live as though part of a different world.

When you employ these actions, you will have begun your exodus.

Let us pray:

Father, I pray that you will give your children the boldness to separate themselves from the trappings of this world. We need Jesus to keep us strong and focused on your kingdom. We ask the Holy Spirit to identify those areas that prevent Christ from being formed in us. We trust you and your Holy Word. We ask this in the name of Jesus. Amen.

Review questions:

1. Describe biblical sanctification in your own words.
2. Is it possible to live above sin in your everyday life?
3. What does it mean to "have the mind of Christ"?
4. What steps can you take to develop the mind of Christ?

CHAPTER 6

The Whole Armor of God

Finally, be strong in the Lord and in his mighty power.
Put on the full armor of God so that you can take your
stand against the Satan's schemes. (Eph. 6:10–11 NIV)

AFTER PREACHING THE DOCTRINE OF justification by faith, Paul sat alone
under house arrest. I suspect he was feeling a bit overwhelmed by the
rejection he faced from those he was sent to reach with the good news.
Still wanting to fulfill his mission, the preacher wrote to a newly developed
church in Ephesus. He told them about their new lives in Christ and how
much they should desire to leave their past lives and embrace Jesus. He
also grappled with many issues that were the direct result of the culture
(e.g., marriage, parenthood, and childhood) and a host of other things
that caused even the righteous to struggle. Paul's phrase has become the
hallmark of his teaching: "We are saved by grace through faith."

When Paul described the severity of the warfare in which believers
were engaged, he admonished the believers in Ephesus to recognize the
attitude and devices of the Enemy and to arm themselves with the proper
attitude for victory. "Hmm ..." Paul paused and tried to come up with just
the right imagery to accentuate his teachings. "What can I use to drive

these points home to my fellow believers so they will understand just how dangerous this battle is and will be in the future?"

Just then, there was a knock on his door. It was Marcus, the centurion, who had brought his food.

"Marcus, you may enter, and thank you, sir," Paul said.

As Marcus entered the room, Paul looked at his armor and made a startling observation: the armor of the Roman soldier was exactly what the believer in Christ should be wearing. After eating his meal, Paul sat down and wrote the verses that give us the continual victory in our struggle with our culture.

> Wherefore take unto you the whole armour of God, that ye may be able to withstand in the evil day, and having done all, to stand. Stand therefore, having your loins girt about with truth, and having on the breastplate of righteousness; And your feet shod with the preparation of the gospel of peace; Above all, taking the shield of faith, wherewith ye shall be able to quench all the fiery darts of the wicked. And take the helmet of salvation, and the sword of the Spirit, which is the word of God. (Eph. 6:13–17 KJV)

Wow! He uses incredible imagery to convey tremendous doctrinal truth. Since we are at war, we need to think about our armor and our weapons. Let's look at each item that will help us win the battle.

First, we have the girdle of truth. This is an interesting piece of armor. Our reproductive organs are housed in our loins. This speaks of what comes out of us. Paul teaches that the things that should come out of us must be truthful. The truth is the antithesis of this culture, which is built on lies. So, for the child of God, battling for the truth is a daily struggle. As true believers, we must be sure that truth regularly springs from our loins. The truth is the essence of God, and since we are his children, we must be truthful as well. In this lying culture, we must be beacons of truth!

The second piece of armor is the breastplate of righteousness. Your heart, lungs, and other vital organs are located in the chest area. Paul teaches that we must protect our vital parts with righteousness. In short, we must protect our relationship with the Lord Jesus in our hearts. When our hearts are right before God, our actions will follow.

After his sin with Bathsheba was exposed, David cried, "Create in me a clean heart, O God; and renew a right spirit within me" (Psalm 51:10 KJV). He wanted to return to the heart of God. In the same way, you must guard your heart against all that this culture tries to inject into it. Our hearts should promote true worship and a desire to obey God, as the following verse says: "Now therefore put away, said he, the strange gods which are among you, and incline your heart unto the LORD God of Israel" (Joshua 24:23 KJV). Joshua was telling the children of Israel that they should abandon the culture and yield their hearts to the Lord. Laying aside our false gods and yielding our hearts to the Lord is the challenge we face today. We must purge ourselves of the things that alienate us from Christ and cause us to embrace the culture. Are you wearing your breastplate of righteousness?

The third piece of armor covers our feet. Paul says, "Having your feet shod with the preparation of the Gospel of peace." The word *shod* means to "bind up or equip." It speaks to Christians using their feet to spread the gospel. Have your feet ever carried you to mischief? Now, our feet are bound to the message of Christ, and the Lord is using our feet to promote the good news about his divine Son, Jesus! Praise the Lord! How is this part of the defensive armor we must wear? The best defense is a swift offense. If we use our feet to carry the message of Christ, the Enemy will have to spend his time trying to stop an unstoppable message rather than bringing division to the Lord's church. If our feet carry us to prayer instead of gossiping and backbiting sessions, we will see a true move of God in our churches. It is easy to understand why Paul speaks of our feet.

I should add one interesting characteristic regarding the shoes of the Roman soldier. The soles of their sandals had little spikes on them to keep troops from slipping backward in battle. The spikes gave them traction. If we keep moving forward in this fight, our King will provide all the traction we need to win. Our culture will prevent us from moving forward if we look at the things behind us rather than the victory down the road. Keep looking and moving forward. When I was in the marines, a sergeant told us that if we kept our heads and eyes toward the front, we would get there eventually. Interesting, isn't it?

So you are in the battle now, and you are standing with the correct protection for your loins, chest, and feet. Here comes the Enemy, and you think you are ready. Not so fast. You also need a shield, which Paul calls "the shield of faith." The soldier that Paul used as a reference probably carried a combat shield, which was about twenty-four inches in diameter and had a leather strap in the back. It was usually made of metal and not very heavy. I am sure you've seen one in old movies. It worked, but it had flaws. After a while, the soldier's arm became weary and the shield dropped, leaving him vulnerable. This type of shield speaks about our fleshly faith. Faith that is built on religion and works is small and tiring. It can provide a degree of protection, but it offers no real peace of mind. Is this the type of shield you want to carry into battle?

Roman legionnaires carried a different kind of shield. Called a *siege shield,* it was larger and covered the entire upper half of the soldier's body. Usually, it was made of a heavier material, most likely wood, and it could be forced into the ground for an extended battle. It was also covered with leather, so when the enemy launched flaming arrows, the shield just absorbed the heat. In the same way, Paul says the shield of faith will extinguish the fiery darts of the wicked. When the Enemy throws doubt and fear at us, the shield of faith will repel those darts and help us stand in Christ. Below are some verses that speak about the importance of faith.

> For therein is the righteousness of God revealed from faith to faith: as it is written, the just shall live by faith. (Rom. 1:17 KJV)

> Therefore being justified by faith, we have peace with God through our Lord Jesus Christ. (Rom. 5:1 KJV)

> Not for that we have dominion over your faith, but are helpers of your joy: for by faith ye stand. (2 Cor. 1:24 KJV)

> For we walk by faith, not by sight. (2 Cor. 5:7 KJV)

The shield of faith is vital for our daily life as Christians. This culture breeds doubt and unbelief. Everywhere we look we see some kind of conflict that causes us to think that maybe the Lord is not who he says he is. There is so much sickness and disease that we wonder if Jesus is truly the Lord, who heals. During these times, we must use our shield of faith and move forward. We must not allow what we see to determine our future with the Lord. I urge you to drop that little shield of human reasoning and pick up the shield of faith!

Paul said there is one more piece of defensive armor that the child of God absolutely must have—a helmet. This will keep your mind stabilized. This is important because the principle battle is for control of the mind. The mind is the most fertile ground we possess.

When I was a child, I suffered from bad dreams. One on occasion, my dream was particularly oppressive. It was about monsters coming to get me. I went into my parents' bedroom, crying. My mother assessed my condition, and then she gave me this advice: "Go back to bed, and think about birds singing and the beauty of flowers." I believe that her advice was designed to help me redirect my thoughts. Can you believe that little bit of advice worked? It still works today. Our Enemy knows that whoever controls our minds will control our actions as well.

Paul addresses mind battles in his letter to the Corinthians.

> For the weapons of our warfare are not carnal, but mighty through God to the pulling down of strong holds. Casting down imaginations, and every high thing that exalteth itself against the knowledge of God, and bringing into captivity every thought to the obedience of Christ. (2 Cor. 10:4–5 KJV)

In this passage, Paul tells us to cast down imaginations, which means reasoning or thoughts. He also tells us to reject every imagination that is contrary to the Word. This is a crucial battleground for the Enemy. If he can get us to imagine our defeat, he has already gained the victory. You must cast down and reject as a lie all the imaginations of defeat that the culture brings your way. You are more than a conqueror, even if you do not see it in the natural. You must reject the contrary ideas the Enemy brings your way on a daily basis.

Next, Paul tells us to bring into captivity every thought that exalts itself against what we know about the Lord. Now listen: some things are just not open to debate. When you have this type of conviction in your mind, it is very difficult for anyone to challenge you. Your relationship with Jesus should be established on the Word of God and the belief that what he has spoken is true. Earlier in this chapter, I encouraged you to guard your heart. You must also guard your mind and keep Satan out of it. Here's one more bit of instruction regarding the mind: "Finally, brothers, whatever is true, whatever is noble, whatever is right, whatever is pure, whatever is lovely, whatever is admirable--if anything is excellent or praiseworthy--think about such things" (Phil. 4:8 NIV). We must keep our minds filled with positive and godly thoughts. We must think about the things that are right and good. The Bible teaches us that we are what we think. Can you imagine that? So let today be the day you determine to think like the victorious person you are. Positive thoughts yield positive actions. As the godless culture confronts you, discipline your mind to the purpose of the Lord to bring him honor and glory. The challenge we face is to develop a proper thought life, and we simply must be victorious in this endeavor.

As Paul finishes his list of armor for the children of God, it becomes clear that we have an abundance of defensive weaponry. Yet no one wins a battle against so great an adversary without some offensive weapons. Paul recalls, once again, the weapons that the centurion was wearing, and it comes to him in a flash—a sword! This is a key weapon that every child of God must have. Let's call it the "sword of the Spirit." With it, you will be able to make advances in the spiritual realm. Some will excel in this area because they enjoy the thrill of battle. They live for conflict! I call this the "Joshua spirit."

In my early days as a Christian, I had such a spirit. I loved to engage the culture and introduce Christ to the darkened world. One time during my ninth grade mechanical drawing class, our teacher left the room, and I found myself with about twenty young men who, in my estimation, were on their way to hell. I was not going to let that happen without a fight! I stood up and preached what I knew. Keep in mind that I had been saved for all of thirteen hours! Yet I had this burning desire to tell them about my Jesus. As I stood and shared what I had heard my pastor say the day before, guess what happened? Some of them fell under conviction as the Holy Spirit planted seeds in them that he would use as they grew up to become men of God.

We do not see much of this warrior attitude today. We have become fat, lazy, and complacent in our walk with the Lord. It seems as though our passion for the things of God has been replaced by blessings and the pursuit of worldly honor. Our culture has produced so many things that are designed to please and manipulate us into inactivity. Sadly, it seems that real warriors of the Lord are gone. It is a classic military move, and we have fallen for it without realizing the results of the actions. Whenever our Enemy seems to be at peace with us, we are probably falling into a trap. This strategy has worked down through the centuries. Satan is the master of using deception through prosperity. Here are some examples of how this tactic was used both in the Bible and in history:

- Samson and Delilah: When his enemies could not kill Samson, they used a woman to put him in a position of compromise and weaken his anointing.
- David: Although the man killed a giant on the battlefield, he fell to his own passions.
- The army of Troy: When the Greeks could not penetrate the walls of Troy, they left a horse made of wood outside of the gates. The Trojans brought the horse inside. The Greek soldiers were carefully hidden inside the wooden horse. Later, the Greeks opened the doors for their army. The Trojans' pride caused them to bring the horse inside, which helped the Greeks take over their city.

Paul calls the Word of God the Sword of the Spirit and believe me, it is powerful! When Jesus was confronted by Satan in the wilderness, he did not fight him with anything but the Word of God. In response to each one of Satan's temptations, Jesus spoke these powerful words: "It is written." We can do the same thing. Just tell the Enemy, "It is written," which will force him to withdraw. However, only those connected to the Lord will be able to use the sword. Good swordsmanship also requires practice. Therefore, you must study the Word to keep yourself sharp. You must also surround yourself with sparring partners, other Christians who believe the Word of God is powerful.

Soldiers wore their swords on their hips so they were always in reach. Their lives depended on being able to grab their swords quickly if the battle was thrust upon them. Since the sword is a metaphor of the Word of God, we must keep the Word close to us so we can defeat our ever-present Enemy, just as the psalmist says. "Thy word have I hid in mine heart, that I might not sin against thee" (Psalm 119:11 KJV). When we commit God's word to heart, sin will not come so readily. We also remain in daily communication with our commander. His Word is precious, and as we read, study, and obey the Word of God, we find strength and nourishment for our souls.

This culture tries hard to remove the Word of God from its place of honor in the world. For many centuries, the Enemy has launched many attacks against the Bible. Yet it remains a national bestseller, and many still find comfort from it. As long as we remain faithful to the Word, we will walk in victory. So keep that sword sharp and ready for battle!

Let us pray:

Lord Jesus, we ask for your divine grace and help as we stand against Satan's devices. Please help us to stay clothed and vigilant as we stand against this culture. Amen!

Review questions:

1. Have you lost the passion to reach the lost for Jesus? If so, why?
2. Like the city of Troy, has Satan been able to infiltrate your life and bring you to destruction?
3. Can you identify the areas of weakness and worldly influence that seek to weaken your walk with the Lord and strip you of your power?
4. How can you break free from these attacks and protect yourself in the future?

CHAPTER 7

Cultural Giants

And they returned from searching of the land after forty days. And they went and came to Moses, and to Aaron, and to all the congregation of the children of Israel, unto the wilderness of Paran, to Kadesh; and brought back word unto them, and unto all the congregation, and shewed them the fruit of the land. And they told him, and said, we came unto the land whither thou sentest us, and surely it floweth with milk and honey; and this *is* the fruit of it. Nevertheless the people *be* strong that dwell in the land, and the cities *are* walled, *and* very great: and moreover we saw the children of Anak there. The Amalekites dwell in the land of the south: and the Hittites, and the Jebusites, and the Amorites, dwell in the mountains: and the Canaanites dwell by the sea, and by the coast of Jordan. (Numbers 13:25–29 KJV)

I HAVE ALWAYS HAD DIFFICULTY understanding this story. The children of Israel had survived four hundred years of Egyptian bondage and then watched the mighty hand of God deliver them from Pharaoh's pursuing armies. They had been fed miraculously by God's hand and seen his glory cloud. You'd think they would have been able to rest in God's presence. But when they were just a few miles from the Promised Land, they became frightened by a few measly giants and warrior tribes. They were about to walk into their inheritance, yet they let an outside force keep them from the blessings of God. Have you ever experienced something similar in your life? I must confess that I have done the same thing at times; I've looked at the giants and missed the move of God. While I am amazed by the response of the Israelites, I can also sympathize with them.

In this confusing culture, it is easy to become fearful and doubtful regarding the promises of God. For example, these questions tend to roll around always in our minds.

- Is this God's will for my life?
- Has the Lord given me a direct answer?
- Why aren't things going in the direction I expected?
- Why am I alone in this world?

These are all valid questions, and we should take our requests to the Lord so his peace can rule in our hearts. Yet I am sure you will ask these questions, look at the "giants," and doubt God's abilities. After all, it is only natural, but we are called to be supernatural. You have been called to serve the Lord in a culture that is anti-Christ. We must recognize the cultural giants that prevent us from the best life we can live for the Lord. We are on the threshold of a great move of God. He has promised to restore what the Enemy has taken and prepare his people for a great revival, but this won't happen if we keep looking at the giants instead of the Lord of Hosts!

When the children of Israel saw the giants, they were afraid. So much had happened over the last few years—frogs, lice, darkness, bloody water, and then, of course, death. Their heads were probably spinning with both delight and confusion. They had witnessed the ultimate miracle: the opening of the Red Sea and the end of the pursuing Egyptian army. They had endured battles with marauding bands of Amalekites, and let's face it; they were tired. Living by faith is not easy, even for those of us with a complete Bible. Imagine what it was like to exercise faith in the middle of a hot, steamy desert. I can sympathize with the Israelites as they finally wandered into the Promised Land, only to find it inhabited by giants, warrior nations, and people who were bent on stopping their advance. Let's not judge them too harshly as we evaluate the situation. However, as a result of these obstacles, they decided they could not enter the land that was theirs. They simply could not get past the giants.

As we move toward the Lord's goal for our lives, we face giants as well. The giants that plague our culture are just as frightening as the Amalekites. Our Adversary—Satan—uses the giants of our culture to destroy us, and often we are blind to his assaults. We can become just as tired as the children of Israel became in the wilderness because we must also process many things during our walk with the Lord. Just as they faced particular enemies, we must identify our enemies and the things that keep us in a state of doubt. Let's examine some of the most significant giants of our culture and how we can overcome them.

Giant 1: Sexual Compromise

> While Israel was staying in Shittim, the men began to indulge in sexual immorality with Moabite women, who invited them to the sacrifices to their gods. The people ate and bowed down before these. So Israel joined in worshiping the Baal of Peor. And the LORD's anger burned against them. (Num. 25:1–3 NIV)

When the Prophet Balaam could not curse Israel, he suggested to the King of Moab that the people of God would curse themselves by interacting with the Moabite women—and he was right! By joining with the daughters of Moab, the children of Israel committed sexual immorality with the people of Baal-Peor. This is always the way of our Enemy. He tries to bring the people to a place of immoral satisfaction, and then he causes them to bow down. As a result, they incur God's wrath.

Like the children of Israel, we have engaged in a lascivious lifestyle, and we have lost our ability to affect change in the world. Sex, sex, and more sex! This culture is a breeding ground for illicit sex. In the days of my youth, the sexual revolution was just beginning, and our culture was not prepared for the actions that followed. It was a drastic revolt against the disciplines and traditions to which we baby boomers had become accustomed. The country was still reeling from the assassinations of President John F. Kennedy, Dr. Martin Luther King, and Senator Robert Kennedy. The war in Vietnam had torn us apart, and people were looking for ways to rid themselves of the stress that came along with everyday life. Many turned to sex, drugs, and a new style of music that was clearly designed to send a message of revolt and distrust to the government. What was once a sacred bedroom activity was brought into the open. Lewdness and pornography became entirely acceptable. Hiding behind a misinterpretation of the First Amendment, pornographers distributed their smut freely. I recall the days when raunchy magazines were kept behind the counter and the people who bought them hid them in paper bags. That all began to change in the 1960s.

The church spoke against these changes and challenged Christians to abstain from this behavior, which was clearly designed to weaken our corporate anointing. We put up a good fight for a while, but then the things people had to stand in line to see became available in our homes. DVDs, cable, and satellite television brought not only the gospel into our homes but also the tools of Satan. As a result, the church began to lose this cultural battle. Pastors preached holiness, but then many of our congregants—and many of the pastors!—went home and engaged the cultural giant of pornography on television and the Internet.

When I became a Christian, I was warned to avoid the things that would keep me from being used by the Lord to destroy the kingdom of darkness. Yet, the individuality of the 1970s brought a new attitude to the church. Christians lost their desire for holiness and began to look for Scriptural loopholes. Many seemed to bend as many of God's rules as they could. The result was a lessening of real intimacy with the Lord. Just as America was going through a cultural upheaval, the church was struggling to understand why the Lord was not allowing them to have fun. When we began to connect with "Moab" in this way, we lost something. Balaam could not curse the children of God, yet they could curse themselves. Since we have gone the way of Moab, it is just a matter of time before we fall to the trappings of Baal and lose our power to influence the world.

We must return to biblical purity and holiness. We do not hear much preaching about holiness anymore, but I am convinced that holiness is still the right thing to pursue. We often hear about the Psalms of praise, yet we forget about the Psalms of holiness. For example, "Wash me thoroughly from mine iniquity, and cleanse me from my sin" (Psalm 51:2 KJV) and "Wherewithal shall a young man cleanse his way? By taking heed thereto according to thy word" (Psalm 119:9 KJV). David wanted to praise the Lord with a clean heart. Do you desire the same type of heart? Then we must defeat this giant of sexual compromise that has infested the church of the living God. How do we do it? Simple: Return to the Lord and practice the doctrine of holiness. We must set standards that are in line with the pure Word of God and not allow human minds to change what God has said. Historical studies reveal that sexual perversion is one of the things that led to the downfall of the great Roman Empire. Paul addresses this perverse attitude in Romans 1.

> The wrath of God is being revealed from heaven against all the godlessness and wickedness of men who suppress the truth by their wickedness, since what may be known about God is plain to them, because God has made it plain to them. For since the creation of the world God's invisible qualities—his eternal power and divine nature—have been clearly seen, being understood from what has been made, so that men are without excuse. For although they knew God, they neither glorified him as God nor gave thanks to him, but their thinking became futile and their foolish hearts were darkened. Although they claimed to be wise, they became fools and exchanged the glory of the immortal God for images made to look like mortal man and birds and animals and reptiles. Therefore, God gave them over in the sinful desires of their hearts to sexual impurity for the degrading of their bodies with one another. They exchanged the truth of God for a lie, and worshiped and served created things rather than the Creator—who is forever praised. Amen. Because of this, God gave them over to shameful lusts. Even their women exchanged

natural relations for unnatural ones. In the same way the men also abandoned natural relations with women and were inflamed with lust for one another. Men committed indecent acts with other men, and received in themselves the due penalty for their perversion. Furthermore, since they did not think it worthwhile to retain the knowledge of God, he gave them over to a depraved mind, to do what ought not to be done. They have become filled with every kind of wickedness, evil, greed and depravity. They are full of envy, murder, strife, deceit and malice. They are gossips, slanderers, God-haters, insolent, arrogant and boastful; they invent ways of doing evil; they disobey their parents; they are senseless, faithless, heartless, ruthless. Although they know God's righteous decree that those who do such things deserve death, they not only continue to do these very things but also approve of those who practice them. (Rom. 1:18–32 NIV)

The breakdown of the knowledge of God and refusing to obey his Word led to judgment. Even though Rome was a successful military and political nation and political nation, it lacked moral and spiritual purity. This resulted in the empire's collapse. I believe America is on the same disastrous course. We have become vulnerable in many areas of our country because we have become promiscuous. Now it is up to the body of Christ to lead the way back to purity and godliness. Here are a few simple steps that will help us kill this giant.

Step 1: Keep your mind on the things of God.

Finally, brothers, whatever is true, whatever is noble, whatever is right, whatever is pure, whatever is lovely, whatever is admirable--if anything is excellent or praiseworthy—think about such things. (Phil. 4:8 NIV)

Since the principle battle is for the control of the mind, we can defeat Satan when we think of God and his Word. Never surrender your thoughts to the evil one. Victory will come when we discipline our minds.

Step 2: Keep away from places that do not bring honor to the Lord Jesus.

Solomon tells us that we must not go onto the path of the wicked. I interpret this to mean we should not place ourselves in compromising situations that result in sinful practices. We must avoid these areas and remain on the path that results in God's will being done in our lives. "Do not set foot on the path of the wicked or walk in the way of evil men. Avoid it, do not travel on it; turn from it and go on your way" (Prov. 4:14–15 NIV).

Step 3: Flee sexual immorality.

Your body is the temple of God. Just as we would not live in a dirty, roach-infested house, neither will the Lord:

> Flee from sexual immorality. All other sins a man commits are outside his body, but he who sins sexually sins against his own body. Do you not know that your body is a temple of the Holy Spirit, who is in you, whom you have received from God? You are not your own; you were bought at a price. Therefore honor God with your body. (1 Cor. 6:18–20 NIV)

Giant 2: Love of Money

> For the love of money is the root of all evil: which while some coveted after, they have erred from the faith and pierced themselves through with many sorrows. (1 Tim. 6:10 KJV)

We live in a culture that practically worships money. Paul told Timothy that the love of money is the root (cause) of all evil (1 Tim. 6:10). Money creates greed, which leads to selfishness, paranoia, and low self-esteem. The body of Christ has fallen into this trap, and we need to reevaluate the effect of the money in our lives. Even our leaders have given themselves over to the pursuit of money. As a result, they have traded God's anointing for dollars. I realize some may express concern over my statements, and I appreciate your opinion. However, the truth is clear, and we have to acknowledge the fact that the driving force of this culture is money, and that mind-set has come into the church with a vengeance. We live in a capitalistic culture, and we judge the success of others by the size of their bank account and the abundance of their possessions. Unfortunately, we also tend to measure God's anointing by the size of the crowds and the size of our church buildings. As we read in Isaiah, the anointing carries some concrete proof that we cannot tie into the realm of the material.

> The Spirit of the Lord GOD is upon me; because the LORD hath anointed me to preach good tidings unto the meek; he hath sent me to bind up the brokenhearted, to proclaim liberty to the captives, and the opening of the prison to them that are bound; To proclaim the acceptable year of the LORD, and the day of vengeance of our God; to comfort all that mourn; To appoint unto them that mourn in Zion, to give unto them beauty for ashes, the oil of joy for mourning, the garment of praise for the spirit of heaviness; that they might be called trees of righteousness, the planting of the LORD, that he might be glorified. (Isaiah 61:1–3 KJV)

As we examine this text, we see there is not one shred of proof that the result of the anointing will be a large church with many people. This passage also does not support the theory that the anointing represents money. It does suggest, however, that lives will be touched and people will be delivered if we are truly walking with Christ. As Peter said in Acts, "Silver and gold have I none; but such as I have give I thee: In the name of Jesus Christ of Nazareth rise up and walk" (Acts 3:6 KJV).

This reminds me of a story one of my instructors told our class one day. The church father Augustine was having a conversation with one of his students. While talking, they happened to see some churches that were beautiful in design and material. As they looked at the fancy buildings, the young man said, "Well, my father, as we see these buildings and their beauty, we can no longer say silver and gold we do not have."

Augustine responded, "Yes, we do have beautiful buildings, and we can no longer say silver and gold we do not have, yet we also no longer say, 'In the name of Jesus rise up and walk.'" This is such a great illustration of how we have lost the power of God to get more stuff. The anointing was given to us so we could produce the power of God. With the anointing working through us, we should be able to reproduce the supernatural power of God. We cannot put a price tag on this power. He has left us here to engage in his business until he returns. I find no place in Scripture where we are to put a price tag on the power he provides for us. I am aware that those who preach the gospel should live of the gospel, but was the apostle Paul teaching that the church should help the ministers live in mansions and drive ultra-fancy cars? Have we become carnal and spiritually lascivious to support our luxurious lifestyles? These questions haunt the church as we attempt to reach the masses for the Lord. Our culture has become a breeding ground for teachings that are directly contrary to the Word of God.

> People who want to get rich fall into temptation and a trap and into many foolish and harmful desires that plunge men into ruin and destruction. For the love of money is a root of all kinds of evil. Some people, eager for money, have wandered from the faith and pierced themselves with many griefs. (1 Tim. 6:9–10 NIV)

I cannot tell you how many times people have sought to weaken this verse through various means, yet God's Word is true. Those who are rich will fall into temptations and traps. Paul teaches further that this type of person wanders from the faith and suffers much grief. Now, I can hear the debate escalating: "Pastor Lambert, are you saying we should be poor?" God forbid! The body of Christ should be healthy and prosperous. Yet, I am also in agreement with the apostle Paul as he tells us we should avoid the trappings of this life and lay hold onto those things that will enhance the church. I hope you can help me understand how living in an expensive mansion, driving a luxury sports car, and flying around in a private jet enhances the body of Christ. Paul tells us that our response should be just the opposite of what we are hearing in the world today: "But you, man of

God, flee from all this, and pursue righteousness, godliness, faith, love, endurance and gentleness" (1 Tim. 6:11 NIV).

This culture and its pursuit of riches have caused many unnecessary problems. We have seen the destruction of the home and family as we have fallen for luxurious lifestyles that create massive debt. We have seen what happens when we work longer hours to pay for things we have charged and cannot afford. We come home after working two jobs to pay for them, and then we are too tired to enjoy what we have purchased. We charge and spend, and then when we cannot pay for the things we bought, we borrow more. We are stuck in a vicious cycle.

Against this backdrop, I can hear the voice of the culturally correct preacher telling us to move forward by faith. Buy that large house, buy that fancy car, and go on that expensive vacation. Just do it by faith, and watch the Lord do it for you. This is foolishness! It is time to yell, "Enough!" When will the madness stop? God has not called us to live in poverty or extreme wealth. He has promised to supply all of our needs—remember, our *needs,* not our wants! He will determine what we need, and then he will supply it.

Here is a story about how the Lord helps us to be economically responsible.

> Let Pharaoh appoint commissioners over the land to take a fifth of the harvest of Egypt during the seven years of abundance. They should collect all the food of these good years that are coming and store up the grain under the authority of Pharaoh, to be kept in the cities for food. This food should be held in reserve for the country, to be used during the seven years of famine that will come upon Egypt, so that the country may not be ruined by the famine. (Gen. 41:34–36 NIV)

Joseph told Pharaoh that he should put aside a part of the provision of God and save it for the time when the famine comes. This is a sound principle, teaching others to save during years of plenty so they may have supply during the lean years is an essential discipline for success in life. Believers need to understand this concept and strive to master it. The leaders must work to encourage the people to embrace this principle of economic strength. Money can be a tremendous tool for providing comfort and security, but it can also lead to ruin. Our culture stresses the idea that we must have more money than the Lord says we need. We should trust the Lord and allow him to handle our finances instead. The Word of God provides clear instructions on how we should slay this giant.

Step 1: Live moderately.

Step 2: Do not chase riches.

Step 3: Seek the kingdom of God first.

Step 4: Live within your means.

Step 5: Give regularly to others.

Giant 3: Works without love for God

> Unto the angel of the church of Ephesus write; These things saith he that holdeth the seven stars in his right hand, who walketh in the midst of the seven golden candlesticks; I know thy works, and thy labour, and thy patience, and how thou canst not bear them which are evil: and thou hast tried them which say they are apostles, and are not, and hast found them liars: And hast borne, and hast patience, and for my name's sake hast laboured, and hast not fainted. Nevertheless I have *somewhat* against thee, because thou hast left thy first love. (Rev. 2:1–4 KJV)

Our third giant is somewhat of a paradox for the modern Christian. Often, we are told to "do" ministry, yet in my opinion, we have gone overboard in the works department. It seems that we have become more interested in doing the work of the Lord more than spending time with him. When the church of Ephesus received this message, they were in the midst of a downward spiral that was bringing the church into a form of apostasy. The study of this once great church provides a sad commentary on the twenty-first-century church.

Recall the Ephesian encounter with the apostle Paul in Acts. Paul taught them the importance of the indwelling of the Holy Spirit. While they had experienced the new birth and repentance, they had not moved beyond legalism. Paul prayed for them, and the Ephesians received the Holy Spirit. As the church grew in doctrine and relationship, Paul felt the need to encourage them again with doctrinal teachings that would bring about a sense of fullness and purpose in their new lives. He wrote the book of Ephesians and instructed these believers in the fundamental truths they would need to grow in their relationships with God. However, the people seemed to have forgotten the relationship concept. By the time Timothy became the leader of this once great church, he was confronted with many things that are the direct opposite of the Pauline instructions shared with them in the letter to the Ephesians.

After Timothy had left the pastorate in Ephesus, a new doctrine of gnosticism invaded the church. It taught that nothing good could come from the flesh. Since nothing wholesome could come in the flesh, it showed that Jesus did not come in the flesh, and if that were the case, no one could be saved. Many of the Ephesians left the church and became discouraged because of this doctrine. So widespread was the confusion that some of the people wrote to the apostle John for help. This is why he wrote the books of 1, 2, and 3 John.

By the time we get to the book of Revelation, we see that the church of Ephesus was confused once again about its position, only now the enemy was not a new doctrine or Satan but ministry work. When Jesus sent his message to this church, he called them back to an intimate relationship with him. King Solomon said there is nothing new under the sun, and I believe we are seeing a revived move of our Enemy to bring us into the same form of bondage in which the Ephesians were ensnared—ministry work and the things we do for the Lord. The Enemy is so clever and subtle he uses our very best intentions to lead us astray.

When I became a full-time pastor, I thought I was supposed to be busy, so I joined every ministry fellowship I could and did everything possible to be effective. What I did not realize was that I had simply changed one job for another and that I was just as bound in the work of ministry as I was when I held a secular job. It was awful! Trying to please everyone in the church and give the impression that I was able to work with others in ministry was exhausting.

One day, the Lord called me into a time of prayerful silence, but I was too busy to enter his presence. I was so busy I didn't feel like I had time to prepare my spirit for ministry through prayer, so my preaching lacked depth. I had no idea my desire to be busy and prove my worth was sabotaging my ministry.

I believe we should be about our Father's business, but like the Ephesians, we have forgotten the thing God wants from us more than ministry—intimacy with him! The most frightening development in the church of Ephesus was that they were involved in the works of the Lord, but they had forgotten for whom they were working. We are always encouraged to "work for the kingdom of God." Yet, when we take a close look at our lives, we realize we are actually spending much of our time working on our ego instead. This is a sad commentary on the church today. We work hard so that others think we are busy for Christ when we are not really connected to him at all. We must be joined to Christ more than anything else in our lives. If we spend a considerable amount of time connecting with Christ, we will see the true work of the kingdom is to love the Lord with all of our being. It is easier for us to connect technologically (e.g., through Facebook and Twitter) than to Christ Jesus because it doesn't involve opening up our hearts or being our true selves. But unless we get connected to Jesus, everything we are working so hard to build will fall.

Let's examine the Lord's perspective on this matter.

> And one of the scribes came, and having heard them reasoning together, and perceiving that he had answered them well, asked him, Which is the first commandment of all? And Jesus answered him, The first of all the commandments is, Hear, O Israel; The Lord our God is one Lord: And thou shalt love the Lord thy God with all thy heart, and with all thy soul, and with all thy mind, and with all thy strength: this is the first commandment. And the second is like, namely this, Thou shalt love thy

neighbour as thyself. There is none other commandment greater than these. (Mark 12:28–31 KJV)

Jesus emphasized the most important thing, which is to love the Lord with all of your heart, indeed, your entire being. I can only imagine the scribe as he listened to the scholars of his day discuss the Law of God. As he sat there taking notes and listening to the teachers of the Law argue, he was probably confused and overwhelmed. Each day, he probably left the temple wondering, "Which of these is critical to the Lord?" Then one day the scribe encountered Jesus. Hallelujah! He decided to ask the Lord what was significant to God, and the Lord's answer shocked him. Jesus said the most important law is to love the Lord God with all of your being and then share that love with your neighbor. Wow! What a simple yet powerful answer. I'm sure Jesus disappointed many rabbis and theologians that day. They probably expected him to cover the weightier things of the Law. Instead, this humble carpenter announced that love of the Father was the most important law of all. Then, right on the heels of that revelation, he said they must love their neighbor as themselves.

In light of this, I cannot understand why we spend so much time *doing* for the Lord instead of *being* with the Lord and each other. Throughout my walk, I have been exposed to many "working" Christians. They come in all forms and possess many gifts. Yet, when confronted by the culture and the mind-set of our Enemy, they retreat into the comfortable fleshly realm. This attitude is why Jesus commands us to love the Father first and then each other. Our culture drives us, and now we have become just like those believers in Ephesus. We work for him, but there is no love left for him, as described in Matthew 7:22–23 (NIV): "Many will say to me on that day, 'Lord, Lord, did we not prophesy in your name, and in your name drive out demons and perform many miracles?' Then I will tell them plainly, 'I never knew you. Away from me, you evildoers!'" This is the way Jesus will handle those who allow the cultural definition of Christianity to obscure the truth of following Jesus. Performing good works does not define the Christian life. The real walk of the believer is surrounded by love. Let us work to slay this third and very deadly giant.

Our culture does not embrace love. In fact, this world is the antithesis of love. Instead, it is fueled by hate. We are surrounded by hate, bitterness, and war every day. Jesus predicted this, saying one of the signs of the end times would be the absence of love. "And because iniquity shall abound, the love of many shall wax cold" (Matt. 24:12, KJV). As we are exposed to hate every single day, we literally circle the wagons of our emotions to protect ourselves. This action causes us to respond to the world with the same attitude that we see in the world. Shouldn't the believer be different? Must we always default to the flesh? Have we become so caught up in the world that we miss the will of our Father? Does love really work? These are but a few of my questions as I consider this giant of works versus love.

I hope you do not misunderstand me and assume I do not believe in doing works. Nothing could be further from the truth! Of course, we should do things that reach the lost and build the kingdom of God. In fact, Paul teaches us that pastors must "equip the body for works of service." However, I am concerned that we are turning out *workers for God* rather than *lovers of God*.

As we approach this giant of the culture, let us reassess our position with the Lord and reconnect with his love. We must take on the attitude of David and slay these giants before they hinder our walk or dilute our anointing. David stood up for the Lord at great peril to his own life. Let us do the same. The giants that we see today will fall before Christ if we stand on the Word of God and walk according to his principles. Jesus has called us to a place of intimate service, and we must strive to stay connected to the Lord in everything we do.

Let us pray:

Dear Father, we come before you and ask for your divine help as we try to escape the cultural pull that weakens our faith. We ask that you purify our hearts and bring us back to the cross of Christ for daily cleansing and renewal. Your power gives us the ability to move toward you and become more like Jesus. We resist those things that are contrary to your Word and embrace the teachings of Christ. We ask for your help in all things. We pray this in the name of Jesus Christ. Amen.

Review questions:

1. As a child of God you are called to intimacy with Christ. How would you shape your times of intimacy with the Lord?
2. What are some ways that you can crucify the flesh?
3. Think of the words you speak. Are they motivated by the desire for recognition or love for God?
4. Which one of the three giants described in this chapter is threatening your life? How can you overcome it?

CHAPTER 8

I Do Not Have to Listen to Anyone; "The Lord Told Me ..."

The LORD came and stood there, calling as at the other times, "Samuel! Samuel!" Then Samuel said, "Speak, for your servant is listening." (1 Sam. 3:10 NIV)

THE PARENTS REJOICED IN THE Lord at the birth of their little boy. He was a handsome fellow with brown eyes and a cute little smile. They thought he would lead many to the Lord one day. They named him Saul.

They were correct in their initial evaluation of their son. He was taught the things of God, and he even prophesied. He began to grow, and soon he was a very tall boy. In fact, he became one of the tallest in the town, and there was a definite calling on his life. He spoke for the Lord, and as his gifts grew, he joined other prophets and was very impressive in the administration of his gifting. Others thought he would be a king one day. Saul did not think about such things, though. He only loved Jehovah and wanted to please him more than anything in the world.

After a series of events, the young man was anointed to be king over Israel, and the people of God felt like other nations. Finally, they thought,

"We have a physical ruler among us. Like the other nations, we have a representative that others can see."

Things went well for a while, but then young Saul forgot the God who had called him. He began a series of actions that culminated in these words from the prophet Samuel: "For rebellion is like the sin of divination, and arrogance like the evil of idolatry. Because you have rejected the word of the Lord, he has rejected you as king" (1 Sam. 15:23 NIV). What a difference in Saul's life. How did he go from being selected by the Lord and then being rejected by the same Lord? The key lies in 1 Samuel 15:19–21 (KJV).

> Wherefore then didst thou not obey the voice of the LORD, but didst fly upon the spoil, and didst evil in the sight of the LORD? And Saul said unto Samuel, Yea, I have obeyed the voice of the LORD, and have gone the way which the LORD sent me, and have brought Agag the king of Amalek, and have utterly destroyed the Amalekites. But the people took of the spoil, sheep and oxen, the chief of the things which should have been utterly destroyed, to sacrifice unto the LORD thy God in Gilgal.

Here's another verse that reminds us of how rebellion can end badly: "And Saul said unto Samuel, I have sinned: for I have transgressed the commandment of the LORD, and thy words: because I feared the people and obeyed their voice" (1 Sam. 15:24 KJV). If Saul had obeyed the voice of his leader, he would not have suffered the humiliation of losing his position. What a sad ending to a life that could have been glorious.

Our culture breeds the same sort of rebellion today. In fact, we thrive on it, and we bring it into every area of life. This is the age when we say no one is going to tell us what to do. "This is my life, and I will live it as I see fit." How many times have we heard those sorry words? America is a country born of rebellion. The original thirteen colonies told King George they would not submit to his rule any longer. We even put it in our Declaration of Independence.

Later, in 1860, the South told President Lincoln they would not submit to the laws of unity, which kicked off the Civil War. That rebellion resulted in the deaths of hundreds of thousands of men and women. In the 1960s, Americans told the Lord they would not let him run their lives. Therefore, we kicked him out of our schools, our marriages, and our legal system. We virtually told Jesus we did not want his influence anymore, and whenever he sent us a messenger, we simply ignored him.

Sadly, this spirit of rebellion still infects our culture today. How often do you hear, "No one tells me what to do; I'm free to do whatever I want and free to do what makes me feel good." This statement represents an interesting dichotomy. Yes, you are free to do what you want—as long as you are willing to reap what you sow. We want the Lord to bless our rebellion and enable us to continue in our sins, but God is not going to bless unrepentant hearts. Our culture breeds a spirit of individualism that comes directly from the Enemy of our souls. We are called to unity, not independence. The apostle Paul uses the metaphor of a body of believers. If you notice, there is one interesting fact about a body: it has only one head! However, in the church there is so much confusion relating to submission. Do we submit to our pastors, ourselves, or to God? This is where the poison of our culture takes over and brings sin into the church.

Judges 17:6 (KJV) says, "In those days *there was* no king in Israel, *but* every man did *that which was* right in his own eyes." As our young people are prone to say, "There it is!" The Lord is telling us that when there is no leadership, there will be confusion and sin. If you look at the book of Judges, you will see that the Lord always has one leader to bring order and discipline to God's people. Yet like the people of Israel, the church of Christ has become independent of God's leaders. People do whatever they want and cover it with the phrase, "The Lord told me." I cannot tell you how many times I have heard that phrase used as an excuse for selfish and disruptive behavior. Even in my own ministry, I have had many people tell me that the Lord has told them something, but it was not the Lord at all. They only saw something that they wanted and then used the Lord to justify their carnality. The most dangerous four words in the Christian language are: "The Lord told me." These seven words are equally destructive when placed in the wrong hands: "The Lord said to tell you." When we look at our culture, we see a move to eliminate authority. No one wants anyone to tell him or her what to do. This will result in anarchy and, ultimately, destruction. We see this same mind-set in the church today.

When someone has to be corrected, that person finds it easier to rebel and leave the church.

I recall a story of two married couples engaged in partner swapping. When their pastor confronted them about it, they simply went to another church. No repentance, no sorrow, nothing. They just went to another church so they could continue to do the same sinful things and poison that congregation instead. This kind of behavior occurs when there is no respect for our leaders, and we just do whatever we want to do.

I wanted to do many things as a boy, yet I had a mandate from my parents that superseded my desires. I did not like it, but I knew it was for my sake to submit. Ah, now there is a forgotten word: submission. We cannot submit to God, then rebel against those whom He has in leadership. Our culture does not like the word *submission*. In fact, we would rather rebel because it is easier and it builds pride. We hear phrases such as, "No one is going to tell me what to do;" "I am in charge of my life, and I will do as I want;" or "It does not matter what anyone says; I am in charge." Then a man of God comes and gives this young man the Word of the Lord: "To obey is better than sacrifice." Yes, that young man is Saul, king of Israel, and the prophet Samuel came to correct his spirit of rebellion. That Spirit is in the world and the church today. How can we escape it except through Christ?

Our culture breeds a spirit that refuses to submit to the Lord or his representatives. We see it developing in our children, and as they grow into adulthood, the attitude of rebellion grows with them. There is a complete lack of submission to leadership and biblical authority. Since we are exposed to that spiritual attitude throughout the week, it's hard to escape it on Sundays. That's why we see the church walking in such weakness. People simply refuse to submit to leadership, and it will result in disaster.

Now, I realize some seek to abuse their power. I am not speaking of submitting to that type of leader. I am talking about godly leadership. God's leadership is Christ-honoring and loving.

When the Lord instructed me to plant Bethel, I went to my pastor (Rev. Benjamin Smith) and shared my burden and instructions with him. "The Lord has given me a leading to start a church," I said, "but if you tell me to stay, I will stay right here."

I really meant those words. I knew that my pastor was God's man, and whatever counsel he gave would be the Lord's best for me. Pastor Smith asked for time to pray and then promised he would get back to me.

Two days later, he told me to go forth with my ministry. We had a public send-off, and the Lord has blessed Bethel beyond my imagination. I believe the Lord's blessing is on my ministry today because I submitted to this man of God.

Sadly, this type of submission does not regularly happen in the church today. People feel the need to get on with their ministries even if the Lord has not called them. Our culture is so driven by personal desire and greed that it even bleeds into the Lord's work. We read of this type of attitude in 1 John.

> Love not the world, neither the things that are in the world. If any man love the world, the love of the Father is not in him. For all that is in the world, the lust of the flesh, and the lust of the eyes, and the pride of life, is not of the Father, but is of the world. And the world passeth away, and the lust thereof: but he that doeth the will of God abideth for ever. (1 John 2:15–17 KJV)

Pride and lust are the principle components of rebellion. We want what we want, and we want it now! Isn't it amazing that the apostle Paul tells us we should wait on our ministry? The Holy Spirit was trying to convey the idea that we must develop attitudes of serving before we become leaders. Jesus puts it like this:

> But Jesus called them unto him, and said, "Ye know that the princes of the Gentiles exercise dominion over them, and they that are great exercise authority upon them. But it shall not be so among you: but whosoever will be great among you, let him be your minister; And whosoever will be chief among you, let him be your servant: Even as the Son of man came not to be ministered unto, but to minister, and to give his life a ransom for many." (Matt. 20:25–28 KJV)

The Lord wants us to avoid a rebellious mind-set. It is hard to be rebellious when you have a servant attitude. That's it. Praise the Lord! Now we can see why the Lord Jesus commands us to walk in humility. True humility always seeks to glorify the Lord Jesus rather than bring us into the spotlight. It is time to tear down the stronghold of pride and look to the Lord to help us in all of our ways.

I began this chapter with the story of King Saul. His life started as so many of God's children do, with true humility. Then something happened that infected Saul's mind with rebellion.

> Some Hebrews even crossed the Jordan to the land of Gad and Gilead. Saul remained at Gilgal, and all the troops with him were quaking with fear. He waited seven days, the time set by Samuel; but Samuel did not come to Gilgal, and Saul's men began to scatter. So he said, "Bring me the burnt offering and the fellowship offerings." And Saul offered up the burnt offering. Just as he finished making the offering, Samuel arrived, and Saul went out to greet him. "What have you done?" asked Samuel. Saul replied, "When I saw that the men were scattering, and that you did not come at the set time, and that the Philistines were assembling at Micmash, I thought, 'Now the Philistines will come down against me at Gilgal, and I have not sought the Lord's favor.' So I felt compelled to offer the burnt offering." (1 Sam. 13:7–12 NIV)

Instead of waiting on the Lord, Saul decided that he could perform Samuel's duties just as well as Samuel. The seeds of rebellion were apparently beginning to develop in this situation. As it did with Saul, pride will keep you from waiting on the Lord and compel you to move in your own direction according to your schedule.

Often, the Lord does not respond as rapidly as we would like, so we have two choices. We may choose to wait on him to give us direction or move ahead anyway and assume a role in which we have not received the grace to walk. Sadly, the second choice is the one championed most often by our culture. I have encountered many believers who say the Lord has told them to do something. Yet, when I analyze the matter, it's clear the Lord has not spoken at all. Usually, this type of rebellion is revealed through the following phrases:

- I just have to go and do my ministry now!
- People have told me this is my season.
- I feel such a burning of the Lord's will in my spirit.
- I don't care what anyone says; I am going anyway because I must obey the Lord.

The rebellion begins to "hatch" when the believer thinks someone is hindering his or her ministry. Driven by a sense of emergency, that person runs ahead of God.

I heard this bit of advice several years ago, and I want to share it with you. Someone once told me, if Satan cannot stop you, he will get behind you and push you so fast that you miss the Lord. Often, the fuel he uses to drive us is rebellion. Just look around you; the world breeds rebellion. Like Saul, we desire to live our own lives and follow our will. No longer content to please the Lord, we seek to please people. This is a very dangerous practice.

Often, we find ourselves working to prove that we are called of God. However, the gifts the Lord has given us will work through us eventually. We don't have to force it. Rather, we must seek to connect with our Lord and never allow the prestige of ministry to get in the way of our relationship with him.

Saul allowed himself to become subject to what people thought of him rather than what the Lord declared him to be. One of the subtlest traps of the Enemy is to cause us to become more enamored with the work of the Lord than the Lord of the work. It is the church at Ephesus all over again. In Revelation 2, the Lord condemns the church at Ephesus because they were consumed by the work instead of the relationship. This is something upon which each believer must reflect every day. The work is important and necessary, but it's never more important than the Lord of the work.

If we are not careful, we will wind up like Saul, just doing work for work's sake and missing the relationship the Lord wants with us. Let us strive to connect with the Lord in a personal way and allow the work to be something that we do rather than something that defines who we are. When we are sure of our relationship, we will not succumb to the prideful desire to rise above the Lord's mandate.

Saul stopped loving God and started to put more emphasis on himself and his position more than the things of God. This intense craving for power often leads people to think they hear God, and then they begin to preface their selfish goals and desires with, "The Lord told me!" We must search our hearts continuously to determine if we are really in the will of God or simply chasing our own desires. One of the trappings of our culture is the need to hear from God without accountability, yet I believe that the Lord and his Word call for accountability. We must check everything we hear with those to whom we submit ourselves for spiritual oversight. Remember that "Where no counsel is, the people fall: but in the multitude of counselors there is safety" (Prov. 11:14 KJV).

Let us pray:

Holy Father, please help my heart and mind to become more attentive to your voice. I know that the voice of our adversary has often brought confusion and doubt, but I ask that the Holy Spirit would make your voice as clear as possible. Your Word declares that your sheep know your voice, and they do not follow strangers. I ask that your voice would be as clear as a bell to your children and that you would help us to obey what you tell us to do. I pray this in the name of Jesus our Lord. Amen.

Review questions:

1. How can you distinguish the Lord's voice from the other voices in your life, including yours?
2. Who in your life is in a position to give you correction, direction, and discernment?

CHAPTER 9

We Are the Light of the World

> You are the light of the world. A city on a hill cannot be hidden. Neither do people light a lamp and put it under a bowl. Instead they put it on its stand, and it gives light to everyone in the house. In the same way, let your light shine before men, that they may see your good deeds and praise your Father in heaven. (Matt. 5:14–16 NIV)

A ROOM MAY EXIST IN one of two states: darkness or illumination. Jesus was making this same distinction when he said we are to be the light of the world. The world is dark, so we should illuminate it with the Light who lives in us. We do this by imitating Jesus and demonstrating his love and power. When teaching this truth to the Ephesian Christians, Paul said, "Be imitators of God, therefore, as dearly loved children, and live a life of love, just as Christ loved us and gave himself up for us as a fragrant offering and sacrifice to God" (Eph. 5:1–2 NIV). This is a powerful expression for a child of God. We are called to be imitators of Christ.

I enjoy impressionists. Sometimes, if you close your eyes, it's easy to believe the real person is right in front of you. However, impressionists often use their bodies as well as their voices to imitate celebrities. People are visual and often need to see something to go along with spoken words. This is what the Lord meant when he said we are to do his works as well as speak about him. Let us put two pieces of evidence together. Jesus said, "I tell you the truth, anyone who has faith in me will do what I have been doing. He will do even greater things than these because I am going to the Father" (John 14:12 NIV). This represents the actions we are to demonstrate to the world. It helps us remember what Paul taught the Ephesian believers, that they should imitate the Lord in both word and deed. When we apply both actions and attitudes of love and grace, then our love will be undeniable, and we will shine clearly as lights for him. Praise God!

In these times of spiritual deception, a question comes to mind: Just what is the world seeking from the spiritual perspective? Certainly, religions and doctrines that obscure or dilute Christ have become more acceptable for the people of God. From one point of view, the church has morphed into a social club and appears to be more interested in getting people into the seats than serving the Lord. What was once a typical pattern of action (casting out demons, praying for the sick, evangelizing the world) seems to have been lost in the modern church. It appears that the attitude of being accepted by the world has replaced the need to separate ourselves from the trappings of the world.

Christ has called us to be a light, and in the early centuries that light was dazzling. Yet the light has grown dim and at times does not reflect the person of Christ. We must ask, why has our light grown dim? Have we lost the ability to influence lives and generate a hunger for the things of God? I certainly hope not, but the evidence seems to suggest that the light of Christ is not as influential as it once was. Our churches have become places for worldly events, even though Jesus declares they are to be houses of prayer. I wonder how much time is spent in prayer—I mean *real* prayer. Each and every believer must have an altar and make use of that place on a regular basis. God gave us twenty-four hours in a day. How much of that time do you spend in prayer and Bible reading? Prayer intensifies our light and gives us something to reflect back to the world. Each believer must work faithfully to make prayer a regular part of his or her day. Lights need a power source, and prayer is it. The more we pray, the brighter our lights, which enable us to do the things of Christ.

Let me shift the focus momentarily to church leadership. The characteristics of the church are often a direct reflection of its leaders. If our lights have gone dim, we must look to leadership for the reason. Unfortunately, many who have been trusted with preaching the gospel appear to be more interested in status and competition than kingdom work.

In Acts, the early church had two things that are lacking today: a heart of unity and a spirit of power. The believers devoted themselves to the apostles' teachings, fellowship, the breaking of bread, and prayer. They were filled with awe as the power of God flowed among them and the apostles performed many miraculous signs. All of the believers were together and shared a sense of the commonwealth. They wanted to demonstrate something that distinguished them from other religions. It was uncommon for any group of people to take an interest in the needs of others. This simple act served as a light and an indicator of God's love. Selling their possessions, they gave to anyone as he or she had a need. Each day they met together in the temple courts. They broke bread in their homes, ate together with glad and sincere hearts, praised God, and enjoyed the favor of all the people. The Lord added to their number daily those who were being saved. The outside world was touched by the demonstration of God's love and the power that came from the lives of the believers. Just imagine; one sermon brought over three thousand converts to the Lord!

In one instance, a beggar confronted Peter and John on their way to the temple for daily prayers. This man was doing what was normal for him every day. He only wanted some money for his needs. He received more than he was looking for, as the men of God allowed the light to shine from within their spirits. They pronounced a blessing on that beggar, and he went away rejoicing. I often wonder why we do not see miracles like this in the twenty-first century. Could it be that we are not on our way to the temple for noonday prayers? Is it because we are more concerned with money than spiritual power? I wonder if the church has just become so much like our culture that it lacks the ability to do the things of God anymore. Is it possible that we have become so much like the world that we have lost our distinctiveness and by doing so dimmed our light?

Today, Jesus's statements are more urgent than ever before. We are the light of the world. This implies that people are living in darkness. They are scratching around in the darkness without hope. Jesus gives us these words of instruction.

> This is the verdict: Light has come into the world, but men loved darkness instead of light because their deeds were evil. Everyone who does evil hates the light, and will not come into the light for fear that his deeds will be exposed: "But whoever lives by the truth comes into the light, so that it may be seen plainly that what he has done has been done through God." (John 3:19–21 NIV)

People love darkness because of evil that is resident in their hearts. This is yet another teaching to help us come to a place of grace and mercy. Inherent evil in the human heart is overwhelming. Darkness brings fear and torment. I am sure you can recall a time when you were afraid of the dark. I can remember thinking that monsters were under my bed. When I told my brother about my fears, he told me to turn on the light. Something so simple brought relief to me in my hour of distress! Everything became okay as soon as the lights were on.

Do you see a correlation here? Could it be that many in the world are frightened and confused because the darkness is so prevalent? We have the mandate to eradicate the darkness. Light has a unique ability to chase away fear and bring comfort. This is what Jesus had in mind when he said we are the light of the world. When people are afraid and feeling abandoned by the Lord, we are to be the light that reconnects them with the loving God, who only wants the best for his creation. This is why we are to let our light shine so that people will see our good works and glorify our Father in heaven.

Let us pray:

Father, I ask for your help in these last days. You have called us to be the "light of the world," but my light is being systematically dimmed. I need your help, and I ask the Holy Spirit to direct me in the path you have chosen. I repent for allowing my flesh to dim my light and put me in bondage. I claim victory in Christ and look to him for the help I need. Thank you, Lord, for hearing my petition. Amen.

Review questions:

1. In what ways are you letting your light shine for God?
2. When was the last time someone felt drawn to God through the light of your life?
3. Have you ever struggled with the spirit of rebellion? Are you struggling with it right now? What can you do to overcome it?

PART II

---

*The Major Debates in
Today's World*

CHAPTER 10

Earthly Institutions

SINCE THE CHURCH IS MADE up of people, and those people enter into relationships, it is necessary to evaluate the effect the culture has on those relationships. We have spent a significant period of time developing an understanding of the Word as it relates to individual lives. Now it is vital that we apply those teachings to another critical area: the family and the home.

Our declining culture has had a tremendous impact on the family. Humanistic values have removed the things we once held dear. Marriage has been redefined, and parenthood is under attack by those who seek to remove the necessary boundaries for successful childrearing. The principles of the Word of God are being abandoned, and God is being evicted from the government and homes. There is no more prayer or Bible reading in school. Schools have been forced to install metal detectors to identify students who carry weapons. Once our teachers read the Bible and led the prayer in morning assembly. A primary symptom of the breakdown of the home and family is that teachers have taken on the role of both instructors and parents. The truth of the matter is that the entire system is in need of review. *We need the Lord*! The family is where hope is born. Good things happen when children are raised according to God's Word. The result is adults who abide by godly principles. We are sinking rapidly and losing what was once our foundation: healthy families! We must resist the pull of the culture and hold onto the teachings of God's Word. We dare not continue this slide into secular humanism.

No longer do we look out for one another because it's the right thing to do. Instead, we do only what is in our best interests. We are not willing to fully embrace Christianity, but we are ready to pour out our lives online to people who could potentially hurt us. We forget that it takes time to develop relationships and knowledge. New Christians are willing to do great things in the name of the Lord without learning the Bible or waiting for the Spirit's guidance. It is like wanting to reach the top of Mount Sinai without going through the valley first. The connection between faith and patience started eroding in the 1970s when the world became more automated and people went away from making connections—human and Christian. We have forgotten that there are things worth having faith in, worth waiting for. We have forgotten that the apostles spread the Word of the Lord to people from all walks of life. They went on blind faith that they were doing the right thing for the betterment of their fellow man. The payoff was when people accepted the Lord. The Bible contains many stories where patience and faith led to wondrous outcomes.

Do you recall David returning to Ziklag and finding the village burned and the people taken captive by the Philistines? Instead of rushing after them, David waited for an answer from the Lord (1 Sam. 30:1–4). David gained the victory by encouraging himself in the Lord. He did not allow the current conditions to keep him from giving the Lord the praise. When we struggle with situations that overwhelm us, it is imperative that we learn how to encourage ourselves in the Lord. We cannot wait on people to encourage and support us. We must learn the language of the Spirit and speak what the Lord says about us.

We have to see the value in waiting on the Lord to make us better, stronger. If we wait on the Lord for instructions, we will emerge victoriously and he will make our lives richer. While waiting for direction, we must fill our minds and souls with God's Word. This is an essential part of Christian development. When we read the Bible, God is talking to us, and that brings peace and joy. We dare not forget that the Bible teaches us how to live on earth by God's principles. That's why God gave it to us.

When I was a boy, my parents would leave instructions for my brother and I to follow before they came home. When my friends wanted me to play, they would tempt me to ignore my chores by saying, "Your mom isn't here, so why do your chores?" Despite their teasing, I did my chores because my parents left me instructions to follow so or there would be consequences. And I was afraid of those consequences! I did not take the easy way out or rush through them. I did them as I was instructed and took pride in my work. The Bible does the same thing, giving us instructions on how to live until God comes again.

Today, we want to do things quickly and easily, and the Internet and computers enable us to do this. With so much information at our fingertips, we do not take the time to read and learn from the Bible. Some might consider it a waste of time to use a website that has pertinent information about the Bible. Yet that is just using a shortcut to getting instructions from the Bible. Taking shortcuts have also been ingrained in our minds. We use them for everything from getting directions to doing homework to preparing food. Yet there is no shortcut to being a true Christian. With each generation, the idea of savoring a process or patiently waiting for an outcome has been replaced with one word: *now*. This idea was fueled by new technologies, which have both helped and hurt us. They have made our lives easier and more enjoyable with online banking, smartphones, new medicines, and many other conveniences of life. Yet with advances in technology, the pull away from Christianity has become stronger. We have lost sight of what Christianity is really about.

Christianity is the expression of Christ on earth. We are to be like Christ. We are to read the Bible to see how Jesus dealt the situations and how he demonstrated God's love and concern. Christianity is different from organized religion. Yet in the western world, we have lumped Christianity into a religion for simplicity's sake. That earthly characterization has created a confusing view of Christianity in the broader culture. Now more than ever, we must show that Christianity is truly about living through faith in Jesus and obedience to the words of Christ.

It is easy to become a blind follower of technology through Twitter and Facebook. This action does not work in Christianity. We must engage the Lord in prayer and Bible reading. Many choose to hide behind a computer rather than experience life. We create personas but find it difficult to establish joyful lives in Christ. The earthy institutions that our culture has affected our marriage, childhood, parenting, and relationships.

Let us pray:

Dear Father, help us to keep our family lives in your will. We need you to fill us with your Spirit, and keep our hearts filled with love. Bless our homes with your presence. We pray in the name of Jesus.

Review questions:

1. How are you making Christ the head of your home?
2. Is your family using the Word of the Lord to make a difference at home?
3. Are you willing to try to pray together?

CHAPTER 11

Marriage

For this reason, a man will leave his father and mother
and be united to his wife, and they will become one flesh.
(Gen. 2:24 NIV)

OUR CULTURE HAS LAUNCHED AN attack on the family that has crept
into the church. In the past, the sacred covenant of marriage was viewed
as a special gift from the Lord that was solidified by a lifestyle of honor
and commitment. For centuries, marriage was a type of the relationship
between the Lord and his church. A system of care and concern permeated
marriage life that demonstrated how much the Lord loved his people. The
apostle Paul gave that insight to the believers at Ephesus. He instructed
husbands to love and honor their wives as Christ loves and honors the
church. The wife was to submit to her husband's leadership and not try to
rule over him, just as we submit to Christ.

As we move closer toward the great apostasy (falling away from the
Lord), we see the Lord's plan for marriage unraveling. Our culture endorses
living together and abandoning the once sacred act of holy matrimony.
As a result, the younger generations see marriage as an inconvenience
rather than a sacrament. Sadly, this attitude has come into the church

with boldness. The divorce rate among Christians is as high as among those who are not born again—over 30 percent! If couples cannot afford to get a divorce, they only live in the same house or they separate. The attitude toward divorce is whimsical, with the primary concern being what the couple is losing materially. Questions regarding dividing up assets and child custody take precedence over the love that was lost. The fear of breaking up a marriage and family takes a backseat. This attitude has been fueled by the culture and reinforced by television, movies, and social media.

Here is where my natural pragmatism kicks in. I want to know why marriage and the home have taken such a beating in the Christian community. This Scripture passage may offer some insight on this issue:

> Do not be yoked together with unbelievers. For what do righteousness and wickedness have in common? Or what fellowship can light have with darkness? What harmony is there between Christ and Belial? What does a believer have in common with an unbeliever? What agreement is there between the temple of God and idols? For we are the temple of the living God. As God has said: "I will live with them and walk among them, and I will be their God, and they will be my people. Therefore come out from them and be separate, says the Lord. Touch no unclean thing, and I will receive you. I will be a Father to you, and you will be my sons and daughters, says the Lord Almighty." (2 Cor. 6:14–18 NIV)

This passage gives simple instructions for us to follow as we walk with the Lord. The Holy Spirit teaches that we are to be different from the world. God challenges believers to separate themselves from the worldly system. Instead, we have been so infiltrated by the world that we have become the opposite of what God says we should be. This is most evident in the institution of marriage.

I want to offer hope to those of you who may be struggling in your marriage and/or seeking a sense of direction. You can either choose the cultural response or you can apply God's Word and dare to be different.

One of the most pressing issues facing pastors and counselors is that of finding success in marriage. Many are wondering if this is an obtainable goal. I believe we must go directly to the Word of God for the answers.

Marriage from God's Perspective

God saw that Adam needed a companion, so the Lord created woman and gave her to be the best part of man. She was to bring a sense of completeness to the creation story. The Word of God states, "and the LORD God said, 'It is not good that the man should be alone; I will make him an help meet for him'" (Gen. 2:18 KJV). This was the basis for marriage. The Lord declared that a man was to leave his father and mother and cleave to his wife (Gen. 2:4). This simple action speaks to the ultimate purpose of marriage: complete oneness. Many struggle with marriage today and look for reasons why their marriages are not working. Often, they blame their spouses and look for outside grounds for the breakdowns. In reality, the principle reason for marital breakdown is that couples have forgotten that marriage is a gift from the Lord.

Today, people enter marriage for many reasons, many of which are not in line with God's Word. When it comes to marriage, we must remember one eternal fact: The Lord gave marriage for the purpose of establishing a sound family structure in the world. It is evident that the Lord did not want a man to be alone. Being alone was the only thing in the entire creation process that the Lord determined was not good.

God's design for marriage resonates throughout Scripture and gives credence to the reality of a world that should be populated by happily married people. The apostle Paul gives many passages that instruct us on marriage, particularly in Ephesians and Colossians. He outlines the essential components of a successful marriage to demonstrate the character and nature of the Lord. As simple as it seems, the most important concepts are often overlooked. Paul teaches that the most significant concept is love.

> Husbands, love your wives, even as Christ also loved the
> church, and gave himself for it; That he might sanctify
> and cleanse it with the washing of water by the word,
> That he might present it to himself a glorious church,

not having spot, or wrinkle, or any such thing; but that it should be holy and without blemish. So ought men to love their wives as their own bodies. He that loveth his wife loveth himself. For no man ever yet hated his own flesh; but nourisheth and cherisheth it, even as the Lord the church. (Eph. 5:25–29 KJV)

Paul makes it clear that a husband holds the key to a successful marriage. Love, understanding, and gentleness are the ingredients he must employ. Love and protection are also included with the proviso that a man should love his wife as the Lord loves the church. These are the concepts of having a successful marriage as it relates to men. Women have the most difficult job because they are commanded to submit to their husbands' leadership. "Wives, submit yourselves unto your own husbands, as unto the Lord. For the husband is the head of the wife, even as Christ is the head of the church: and he is the saviour of the body" (Eph. 5:22–23 KJV). He teaches further, "Wives, submit yourselves unto your own husbands, as it is fit in the Lord" (Col. 3:18 KJV). These passages serve as the foundation for a successful marriage. Couples who embrace these principles will find environments of joy and trust in their marriages, but will following them guarantee success?

Two Keys to Successful Marriages

Here is a question of concern to many wives; "How can I get my husband to love me as much as I love him?" Marital success is established when both spouses love each other according to the Word of God. Each spouse brings a unique blend of memories and experiences to the relationship. The couple's response to family and job environments may have a bearing on the way they view marriage as well. Prior to entering into the wedding, each spouse must discover if he or she has hidden soul wounds. Many soul wounds are buried under other emotions, and their damaging effects are subtle. Once you recognize these injuries, you must work to heal them, because if you are unable to love yourself, how can you love your spouse in the manner that he or she desires?

Another factor that contributes to marriage success is good communication, which is not as simple as you may imagine. Sometimes, one spouse misinterprets the desires of the other. It is important to have clear lines of communication. State your needs and desires clearly so your spouse can understand you. Never assume your husband or your wife will always be aware of your needs!

Respect is also crucial. Most couples can comprehend the reality of unconditional love yet lack the ability to understand absolute respect. This causes marriages to undergo difficulty, as both husbands and wives may be incapable of articulating areas of concern to each other. Marriage success requires that spouses respect each other with pure hearts.

Our culture gives the impression that marriage is something to be tolerated or even avoided rather than enjoyed. The perception is that you are better off staying single. I encounter many who share this view. They think it is better for them to be alone than to share a life of commitment with someone who loves them. Those who say that there is no such thing as a happy marriage often validate this view. Yet the Word of God gives the formula for marital happiness and success.

Marital Success *Is* Achievable

A man and wife who desire happiness in marriage should begin by genuinely liking each other. This is the measuring rod for marriage today. It would seem that love is an enigma, and the criteria has shifted from "I love you" to "I like you." This is a new thought in modern marriages, and many suggest that marriages be loaded with positive, affirming speech. In good marriages, people should have as many as twenty positive interactions per day for every one negative one. This is a useful technique to make each other happy. Yet it is not an entirely new idea. The Word tells us how to speak to one another.

> Let your speech be always with grace, seasoned with salt, that ye may know how ye ought to answer every man. (Col. 4:6 KJV)

> A soft answer turneth away wrath: but grievous words stir up anger. (Prov. 15:1 KJV)

> Pleasant words are as a honeycomb, sweet to the soul, and
> health to the bones. (Prov. 16:24 KJV)

People in any relationship desire care and concern. The absence of care can certainly be a cause for unhappiness in marriage. Because our culture thrives on individualism and a sense of entitlement (e.g., What have you done for me lately?), Christians need to reevaluate the goals they set when they got married. What did you expect? Were you whole (emotionally/psychologically) *before* marriage? Did you have a healthy view of your life and the life that God has graciously given to you?

A stable marriage is the foundation of a solid family, which is the basis for our culture and brings stability to succeeding generations. The breakdown in children and teens can be linked directly to the breakdown of marriage and the family. We are to be the light of the world in every area, including family life.

Marriage is designed by God to last throughout a couple's life. Through proper premarital counseling and monitoring by competent counselors, marital success is an achievable goal.

In his book *Making the Most of Your Marriage,* Dr. John C. Maxwell includes six *C*s of a healthy marriage.

- Commitment - Commit to each other.
- Communicate - Communicate with each other.
- Compatibility - Find areas of compatibility and strengthen those things.
- Control - Control your surroundings so they do not control you.
- Consideration - Put the needs of your spouse above your own.
- Coping - Pray and surrender to the will of God.

CHAPTER 12

Childhood and Parenting

THROUGH DIVORCE, POVERTY, DRUGS, VIOLENCE, and even social media, the innocence of childhood is being lost. Today, children are subjected to adult issues in the home, not to mention in the media and on the Internet. When I was a boy, my parents would send me out of the room to shield me from adult matters that could upset me. That does not happen anymore. Parents talk openly about their problems in front of their children because they are too tired and angry to care.

Children can also turn on the television to discover adult issues. For instance, some years ago there was a television show called *How to Catch a Predator*. Predators (male adults) would be set up to meet children for illicit sex acts. The meetings were caught on tape with the host confronting the predators. Children can also encounter such things online. The danger in this is that they will get the wrong ideas from what they see and read and spread them to their friends. There are no longer any safeguards in our culture. Previous generations have created a dangerous environment for our children. We must protect them from being kidnaped and assaulted by strangers, neighbors, and even family members. We must protect them from the negativity that is rampant in our world, especially in the media.

The Word of God tells us that children are gifts from the Lord. They should be cherished and nurtured: "Fathers, do not exasperate your children; instead, bring them up in the training and instruction of the Lord" (Eph. 6:4 NIV). The Bible instructs us on how to pull our families together and undo the damage that has been building over centuries.

It is not only the absence of innocence that affects children but also the lack of faith. We must keep the circle of faith going so that our children will teach the Word of the Lord to their children and so on. By having faith in the Lord, we teach our children to have an unshakable belief in God that will give them guidance, strength, and love, especially in dark times. It will help them form relationships and grow into healthy, confident adults. When the children of Israel were preparing to enter the Promised Land, the Lord instructed them to teach his laws to their children and grandchildren so that things would be well with them and their children forever (Deut. 5). Yet we are witnessing the undoing of that principle in our world. Children are being raised by the television, which is causing many young minds to succumb to worldly pressures. Our children must be exposed to the Word of the Lord as early and as frequently as possible. Then we will see positive behavior come from them.

Children need love and care as well as guidance. Yet our children are being forced to take care of themselves and develop a worldview that is disconnected from the Word of God. We need to return to the simplicity of teaching the truths of the Holy Bible. Then we will see a change in the lives of our little ones.

CHAPTER 13

Relationships

OUR CULTURE HAS AFFECTED THE way we create lasting, positive relationships. By having strong faith, we can build healthy relationships based not on pop psychology but Scripture. People are so eager to follow worldly advice on relationships that they have forgotten they have always had access to God's advice through the Bible. The words of the Holy Bible have stood the test of time and have not become trendy. This can also be true for families, the bedrock of Christianity.

Today's family structure is quite different from that of twenty or thirty years ago when there were fewer divorces and less emphasis on careers. We need to return to raising families based on the teachings of the Bible. Parents need to establish boundaries between their children and themselves. For example, a busy couple works long hours and has a nanny. The nanny acts as a parent, yet the nanny is not able to provide the discipline the child needs, and the child knows it. The nanny does not set boundaries for the child, only reasons with him or her. Some single parents try to be friends with their children from an early age, which sends mixed messages. A child may feel that he can get into trouble without consequences because his "best friend" would never ground him. This sets a child up for failure. Although boundaries can cause friction, they are meant to protect and guide. Christianity has been losing ground because we are too wrapped up in our culture. The church has become a mirror of the secular world. How do we break away? How do we get out of the pop-psychology trap? The answer is that we need to return to the Word of God. We accomplish this in three ways.

The first way is to rediscover the Bible, which is not subject to our culture. In Isaiah 55:8, the Lord says, "My ways are not your ways and my thoughts are not your thoughts." This passage reminds us that his Holy Word is not subject to our time and culture. We must see the Word on a higher level than our world. Jesus said, "My words are spirit and they are life" (John 6:63). The Bible was written specifically to help us navigate our lives here on earth. By studying the Bible, we will see how our lives are being pulled away from God. We will also see how the commandments are meant not to restrict us but to help us live in peace and the Spirit of Christ. We cannot live in the Spirit of Christ if the negativity that plagues our culture bombards us. We will see that we can be happy with what we have and not what our neighbors have. We will also understand what unconditional love truly means, especially since Christ gave up his life for us.

The second way is to rediscover God. Just like rediscovering the Bible, we can actually begin to understand who God is and what he stands for. But first we must ask ourselves, is God real? In pondering this question, we must be willing to open up to God and experience his goodness. We are used to putting up shields to protect us from being hurt and disappointed, which has become a part of our lives. Only when we are honest with ourselves will we be able to be honest with God. We create fake personas on the Internet because we are so afraid to be who we are, who God wants us to be. We must understand that it is okay to be ourselves and even to be alone at times. Christ was alone sometimes, but he was always connected to God.

We also have to ask, can God speak to me? The answer is a resounding yes! He does not talk to us in an obvious way, such as talking on the phone. He speaks to us in many other ways. Some people want definitive proof that God is speaking to them. They say, "If God wishes to speak to me, He can talk directly to me." That is like saying the only way to show love for someone is to say, "I love you." You and I both know there are other ways to show love. For instance, a couple can show love by holding hands, or a father can show love for his son by playing ball with him in the park. We know that love exists, but we have a hard time believing that Christ exists. We would rather put our faith in an idol, a person we only know through the media. We only know this person's public life; we do not know his or her private life. We have no idea whether the individual is a horrible human being off camera. Plus, we pay money to see this person perform, which only gives us momentary joy. We can receive a lifetime of enjoyment without spending money, and the only thing we have to do is believe! It's that simple.

The third way is to work to help someone else, which is a wonderful way to embody God's Word. It is more than doing something physical, such as being a part of Habitat for Humanity or collecting donations for a charity. It is about helping a loved one, a neighbor, or even a stranger in need. One of the best examples of helping others is illustrated in the story of the Good Samaritan. In this particular story, Jesus teaches us how we should care about others and reach out to demonstrate our love and concern.

> And Jesus answering said, A certain *man* went down from Jerusalem to Jericho, and fell among thieves, which stripped him of his raiment, and wounded *him*, and departed, leaving *him* half dead. And by chance there came down a certain priest that way: and when he saw him, he passed by on the other side. And likewise a Levite, when he was at the place, came and looked *on him*, and passed by on the other side. But a certain Samaritan, as he journeyed, came where he was: and when he saw him, he had compassion *on him*, And went to *him*, and bound up his wounds, pouring in oil and wine, and set him on his own beast, and brought him to an inn, and took care of him. And on the morrow when he departed, he took out two pence, and gave *them* to the host, and said unto him, Take care of him; and whatsoever thou spendest more, when I come again, I will repay thee. (Luke 10:30–35 KJV)

The Samaritan gave of his time, talent, and treasure. Jesus was attempting to develop the need to help others. Remember that this man helped when all of the religious people did not. So it appears that caring for people is more important than holding a church title or office.

Helping is not always about giving what is temporary, such as money, food, or clothes. It is about helping someone reach his or her full potential— believing in someone. Empowering someone is a blessing to give as well as to receive. Christ believed in us so much that he gave his life for us. That is such a powerful notion. He was thinking about the whole of humanity, not just certain individuals. We must follow suit and not think about only ourselves, which makes it hard to care about someone else.

This problem is prominent in our culture and seems to have entered into the mainstream of the church. We go to church and make our donation, thinking it will get us into heaven. We are not thinking about the good it does for the church and the community it serves. After all, it's hard to care if you do not know those around you. Prior to the invention of air conditioning, my family would go outside to keep cool and socialize with neighbors. The luxury of air conditioning keeps us shut inside our homes and leaves our front porches deserted. Such inventions, while good, have also separated us from our fellow man, and we must find new ways to reconnect.

Have you ever thought about the concept of serving others? One of the most fulfilling and joyful things we can experience is helping others in their time of personal need and trauma. Identify those you serve and contribute to others in ways that may help them to achieve their goals. I am not referring to those who receive favors from you. Who are you *actually* serving?

Our culture has abandoned the idea of helping, and because of overwhelming stresses and pressures of life, we find ourselves looking out for "number one." This attitude is contrary to God's Word. The Lord calls us a "body of believers," which means we must care for each other. Romans 12:15 teaches us to rejoice with those who rejoice and to weep with those who mourn. This action represents caring and connection. Yet our culture breeds an attitude of individuality. Jesus teaches that the world will know we are his disciples if we have love one for another (John 13:35). This attitude is definitely unique given the mind-set of our world.

We are surrounded by the narcissistic behavior of the masses. "What's in it for me?" has become the cry of this culture. This is so opposite of the kingdom of Heaven.

In the Sermon on the Mount, Jesus teaches that we are different from the world. In Matthew 5–7, Jesus gives instructions that just do not fit into our culture. He teaches that we must avoid conflict, forgive offenses, and bless the person who challenges us and seeks to do us harm. You must agree that this behavior is a bit abnormal. I recall an instance when I asked my congregation to recite a "street rule." I was not surprised as I heard these Bible-believing and Spirit-filled believers quote the mantra of the streets. I said, "If others hit you, you should—"

They responded in unison: "Hit them back!"

Then I said, "If you think they are going to hit you—"

Again, they responded, "Hit them first!" This is clearly not the attitude of service that Jesus taught. Yet it demonstrates the pull of our culture, even to the point of violating the plans and purpose of God.

We must seek the Lord and develop the kingdom's response system. Love, love, love is the master key. The love of God is what separates us from the trappings of today's culture.

Let us pray:

Dear Father, help us to promote true love towards all. Give us the grace to establish a bond of peace and joy in our lives. We ask this in the name of Jesus Christ our Lord.

Conclusion

TODAY'S CULTURE IS THE CULMINATION of several generations that have set what may seem an impossible task of getting back to what it means to be true Christians. We have become trapped in our culture, which has led us to stray from God and the Bible. We are pulled away by false idols and ideals created by the media. We have put our faith in people we have never met. We have gotten away from real conversations and socializing. We do not want to wait for God's grace; we want it now because we live in a society where instant gratification is the norm.

Sadly, our culture has trapped us into thinking we cannot go against it. This is not true. We can break free. An episode of *Star Trek: The Next Generation* features a race of beings called the Borg, who go from galaxy to galaxy devouring planets and cultures. They seem to be indestructible, but Captain Picard and the Enterprise crew try to prevent them from taking over the Federation anyway. The Borg keeps repeating a key phrase meant to discourage Captain Picard from opposing them: "Resistance is futile; you will be assimilated." This phrase comes to my mind often as I evaluate the struggle of Christians within this culture. Is resistance futile? Are we at the mercy of the culture and the powers of Satan?

We are to avoid the trappings of the world and the culture. Paul teaches in Ephesians 6 that we are fighting against principalities and powers and against the rulers of the darkness of this world. We have been called to separation, not isolation. Our Lord tells us very plainly in John 17 that we are to be kept from the evil one of the world, yet Jesus prays that we are not to be taken out of the world. This means that we have the power to live above the cultural trappings that Satan brings to us on a daily basis. Going back to the phrase "resistance is futile," resistance from our culture and its manipulations isn't useless. We do not have to be like the Borg, who worked as a unit and assimilated everyone who was different.

We must have the courage to turn to God and ask him to help us be individuals so we can proclaim our Christian identity. We must get back to simplicity, the sanity of God. We must return to our morals and do what is right despite those who would tear us down. Just as Jesus was brave enough to preach to thousands of people, we cannot let the naysayers stop us. He did not assimilate into his culture; he transformed it. We can do the same. It is possible!

We must stop being victims of our culture and start being the Christians that God wants us to be. He wants us to stop raising our children on pop psychology and start building them on Scripture. He wants us to get to know him, and the best way to do that is to rediscover the Bible. We have forgotten how the Bible can free us from our culture, how it can help us enjoy our lives and receive God's grace. It can help us be the light God wants us to be in the world. We can illuminate the darkness and the evil our culture fosters. My friends, it is time to avoid the assault of the Borg and start being true Christians.

When I thought about this book and the title, it was a bit challenging. After all, I am sure that many in Christ do not see the same challenges I have written about. They are naturally comfortable in the world and their personal Christianity. Yet when I think about how the children of Israel fell to the desires of the land they left, I can see how the church needs to wake up to the reality of sanctification.

I believe this generation has yet to see a genuine, sustained move of God, which is sad. I am a pragmatic person, and I wonder why we do not see the miracles of God performed on a regular basis. I am often challenged by this reality, and I can only reach the following conclusion: Those in leadership are polluting the work of God. It is being sold to the highest bidder. This mind-set is supported by the harsh reality that whoever has the most money and the largest congregation will be on the list for the "better" ministries.

Ministry has become a thing of competition and personal desire. We have seen the decline of truly spirit-motivated worship and watched as the ministry has become a thing of entertainment and amusement. Where is the power of God in all of this? Those who look to seduce both men and women for sexual gratification populate our pulpits, and the need to be a star has replaced the power of Christ. *Where is the power of God?* Our preachers are being exposed as liars and adulterers. People are being consecrated to holy offices, such as bishop and apostle, yet their home lives are not right. Paul said if our home lives are not good, how are we able to direct the church of the Lord. *Where is the power of God?*

Each week, we are being filled with the good news of prosperity and success, so much so that we look at the Lord like a genie in a lantern. Rub the lamp with your tithes and offerings, and then—poof!—God will get you a new car or some other kind of material thing that your flesh craves. *Where is the power of God?*

Instead of reaching the world for Christ, many in ministry simply strive for the accolades of the world. The church has been losing its identity as salt and light. The church of the Lord Jesus has been called out of the world and commanded to separate itself from the world. The command of Corinthians is still very much in effect. The apostle Paul teaches that we must separate ourselves from the trappings of the world that can and will affect our Christian lifestyles. "Therefore come out from them and be separate, says the Lord. Touch no unclean thing, and I will receive you. I will be a Father to you, and you will be my sons and daughters, says the Lord Almighty" (2 Cor. 6:17–18 NIV). I do not believe the Lord calls us to a segregated type of life. However, I do think that we must prevent ourselves from identifying with the world so much that we lose uniqueness.

My father was born in Jamaica and came to this country as an adult. One of the things I remember most about my dad was that he never lost sight of his Jamaican heritage. He never lost his accent or his desire for the food and cultural things he enjoyed while growing up. That taught me something I apply to my life even today. As a Christian, I must never lose sight of who I am, and I must never lose my identity to the culture around me.

Remember the stand that Daniel and his friends took when they were in Babylon? First, Daniel refused to eat the meat that the king's servant served. He remained faithful to the Lord instead. Then his friends, Shadrach, Meshach, and Abednego followed his lead. I am convinced that these are examples the Lord would have us to follow in our daily lives.

Sometimes we will have to take a stand and refuse to comply with the voice of the culture. This action will not always be pleasant, but it is necessary. The name and person of God has come under attack, and it is up to us to make a difference for him. Remember that judgment begins with the house of God (1 Peter 4:17).

It is my desire to raise your consciousness through the things I share in this book. I want you to look at your Christian life, see how much you may have conformed to the world, and then adapt to life instead. I am not a Pharisee; I am merely trying to get you to evaluate yourself in light of Scriptures. I realize there are many trappings in the world, yet I know that the power of Christ can keep us from the world.

Our spiritual fathers and mothers in the gospel took the time to educate us in holiness. I believe they were a bit too strict in simple matters (e.g., hair, clothes, movies, and so on). However, I do believe that they were only attempting to help us develop a lifestyle that communicated the difference between the church and the world. Now, with all the combining and joining with the world, I wonder if their fears have come to pass. Has holiness fallen by the wayside and been replaced by a form of religion that reflects the world? Has Christianity become just another religion and the Lord simply another religious deity? These questions will plague the church until Christ returns. Mark's gospel describes the betrayal of Jesus. While Peter was denying Christ, the maiden declares, "Surely thou art one of them: for thou art a Galilean, and thy speech agreeth thereto" (Mark 14:70 KJV). She identifies Peter's connection with Jesus by his speech. I wonder what identifies you with Christ.

It is time for this generation of Christians to make significant changes in behavior and to demonstrate the person of Christ. We exist to reflect the life of Christ. Do you recall the things Jesus taught during the final phase of his ministry? The Gospel of John says Jesus focused on making his disciples (present and future) function as one. He stressed that the oneness and unity should model the oneness between himself and the Father. I often think about that prayer, and I am blessed by his words: "Father, make *them* one as *we* are one." This tells me that our lives and our churches must reflect the life of the Godhead. This is a real awesome responsibility to assume. In light of this priestly prayer, we must never allow the culture to extinguish the fire of the Holy Spirit. We must remember that we exist in Christ. We have been crucified with Christ, and our present life is dedicated to Christ.

We must continue to look to the Lord to bring us into a place of sacrifice and rest. I wrote this book to bring Christians into a place of sanctification and holiness that reflects the Lord. Let's keep our eyes on him and not allow the culture to remake us in the image of the world.

I pray that the Spirit of the Lord God will keep you moving toward the glory cloud of his presence.

Blessings

About the Author

BISHOP ERIC A. LAMBERT JR. received training and mentoring for his ministry from Pastor Benjamin Smith of Deliverance Evangelistic Church of Philadelphia, PA. Bishop Lambert lives out his conviction that the greatest commandment is to love the Lord with all of one's heart; he challenges Christians to renew their passion for the Lord.

Bishop Eric A. Lambert, Jr serves as the Senior Pastor of the Bethel Deliverance International Church, in Wyncote, PA. Bethel is a growing church that seeks to promote the deity of the Lord Jesus. Bishop Lambert believes that the church should be a place where the glory of the Lord resides so that hungry men and women can find eternal life through Christ and be at peace with God.

Printed in the United States
By Bookmasters